Yosemite

Capturing Nature's Grandeur

Yosemite National Park, nestled in the heart of the Sierra Nevada Mountains, stands as a testament to the unparalleled beauty and power of the natural world. From the towering granite cliffs to the serene meadows, from the thundering waterfalls to the delicate alpine flora, Yosemite's diverse ecosystems create a symphony of colors, textures, and life that has inspired generations of adventurers, artists, and explorers.

As you turn each page, we hope you'll find inspiration in the raw beauty that Yosemite unfurls, an inspiration that sparks a renewed commitment to preserving and cherishing our planet's natural treasures. Join us as we journey through the seasons, the landscapes, and the emotions that define Yosemite – an ode to nature's grandeur that words alone could never fully convey.

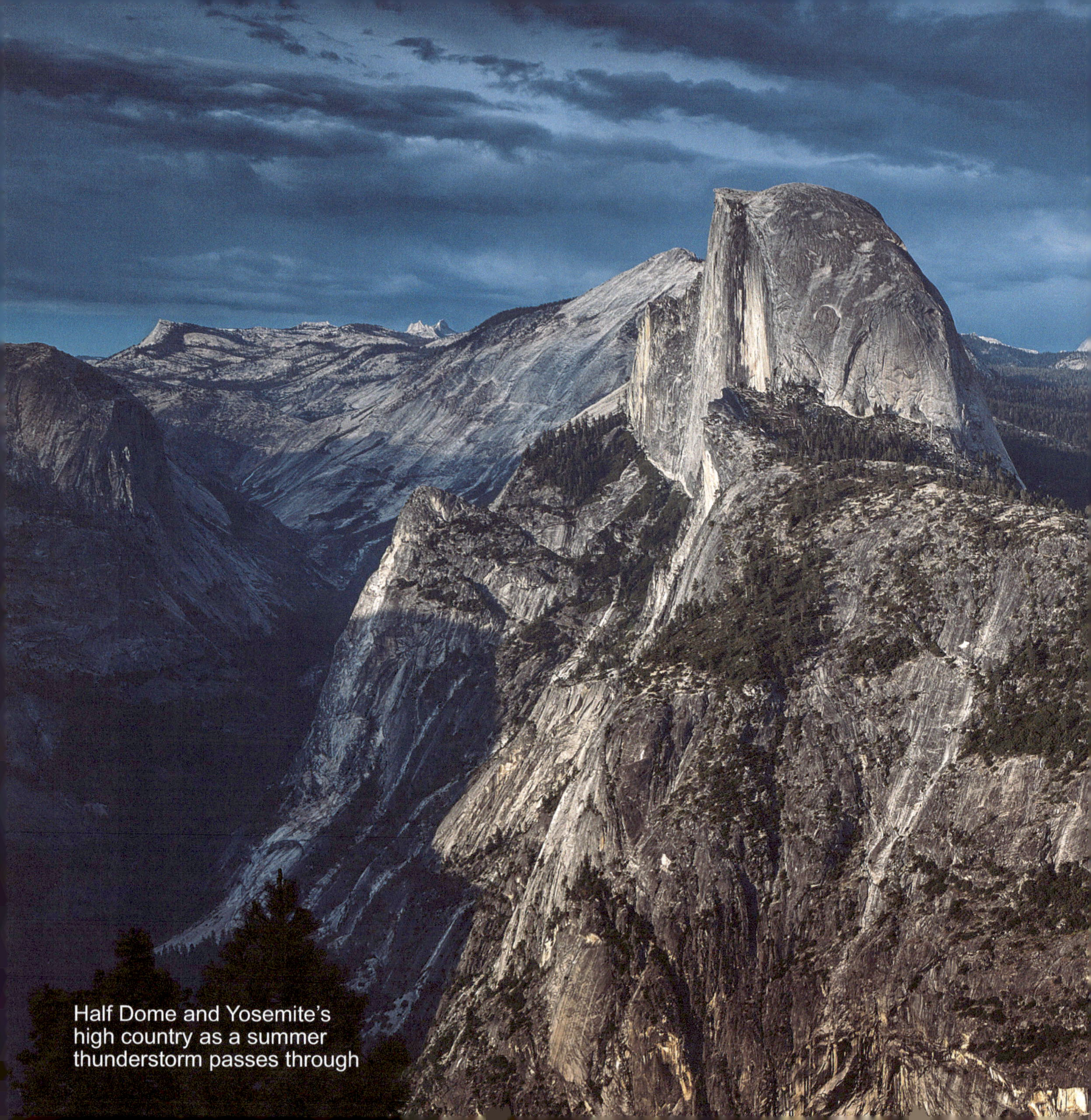

Half Dome and Yosemite's
high country as a summer
thunderstorm passes through

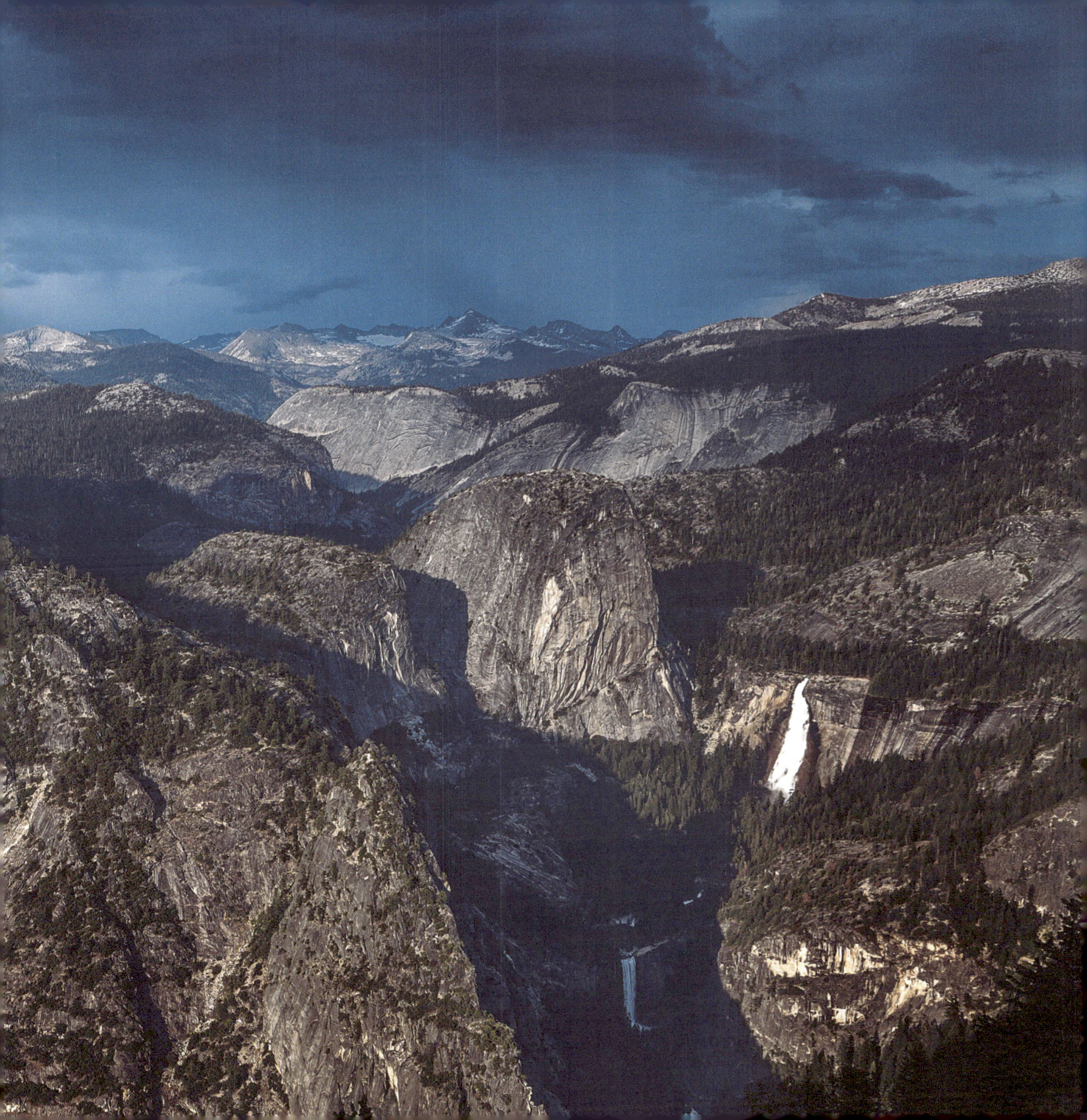

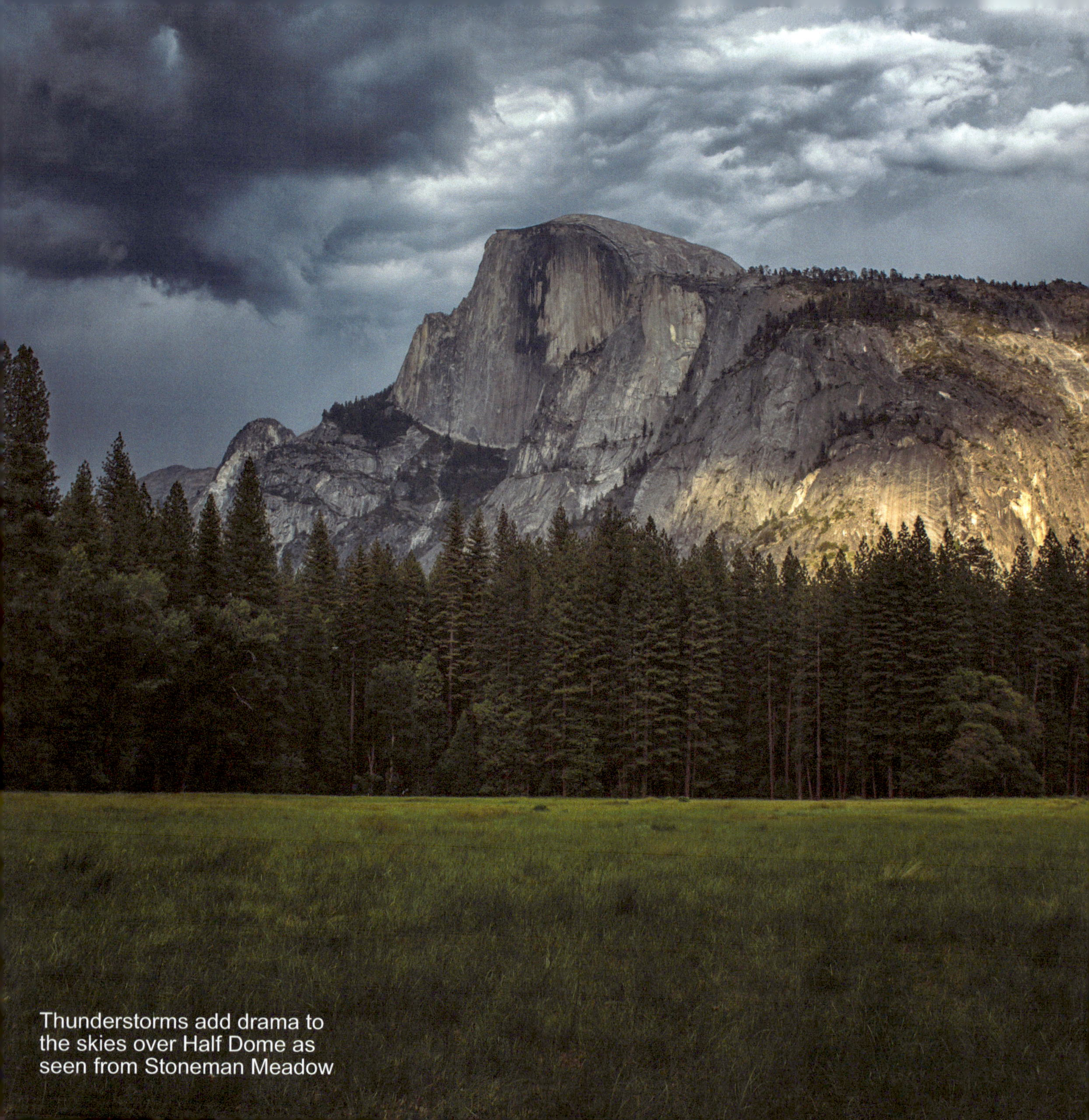

Thunderstorms add drama to
the skies over Half Dome as
seen from Stoneman Meadow

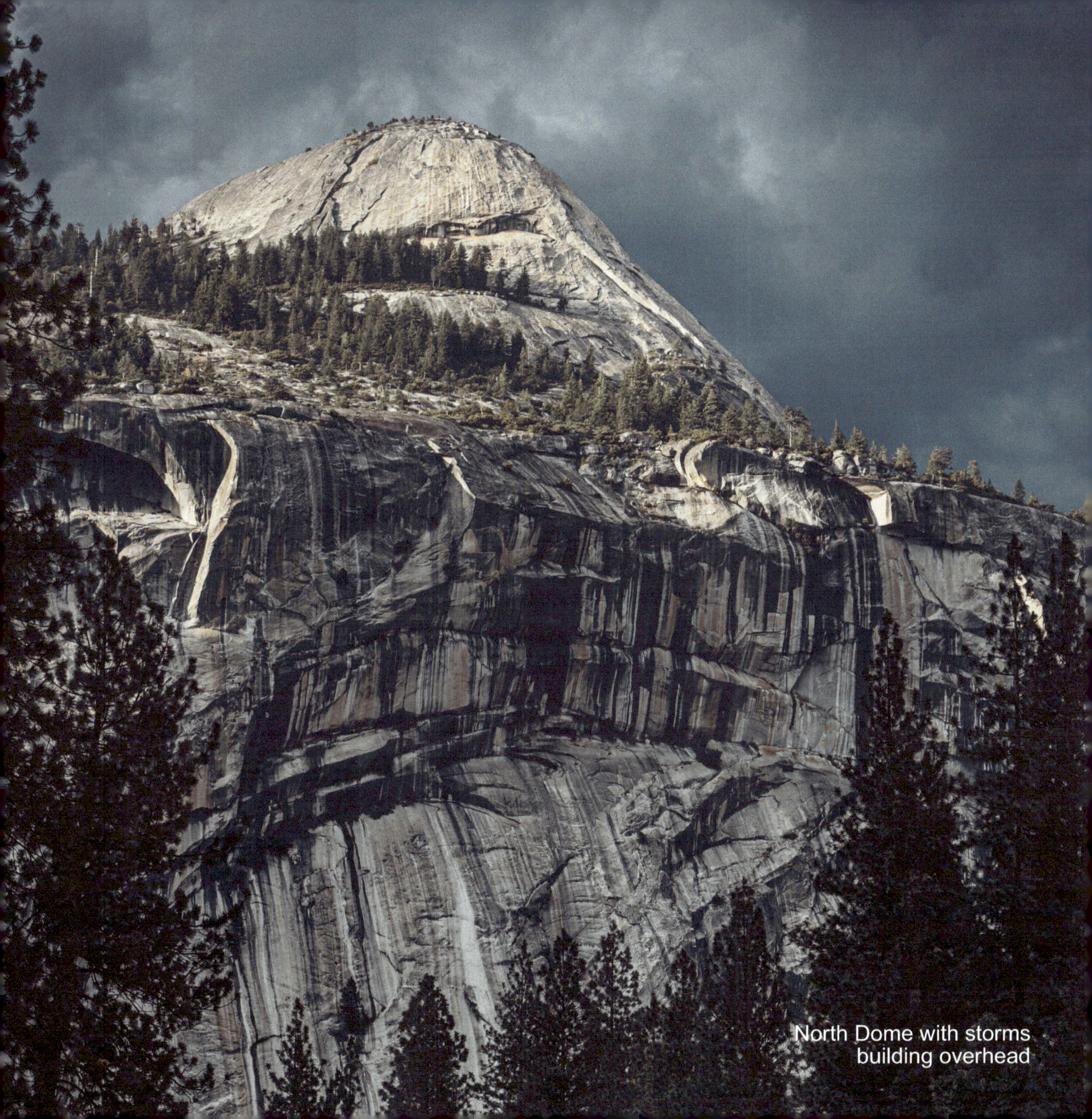

North Dome with storms
building overhead

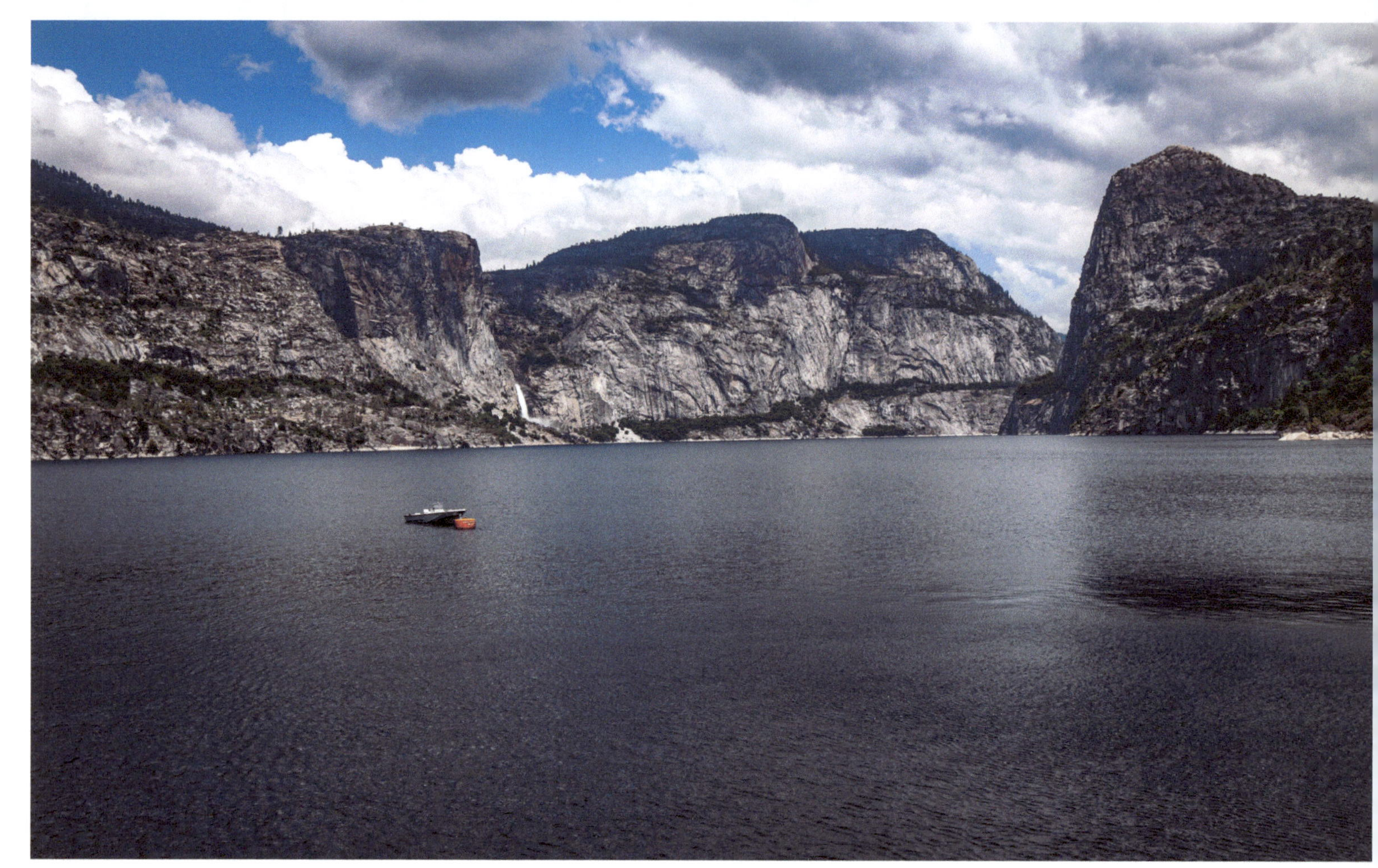

Hetch Hetchy

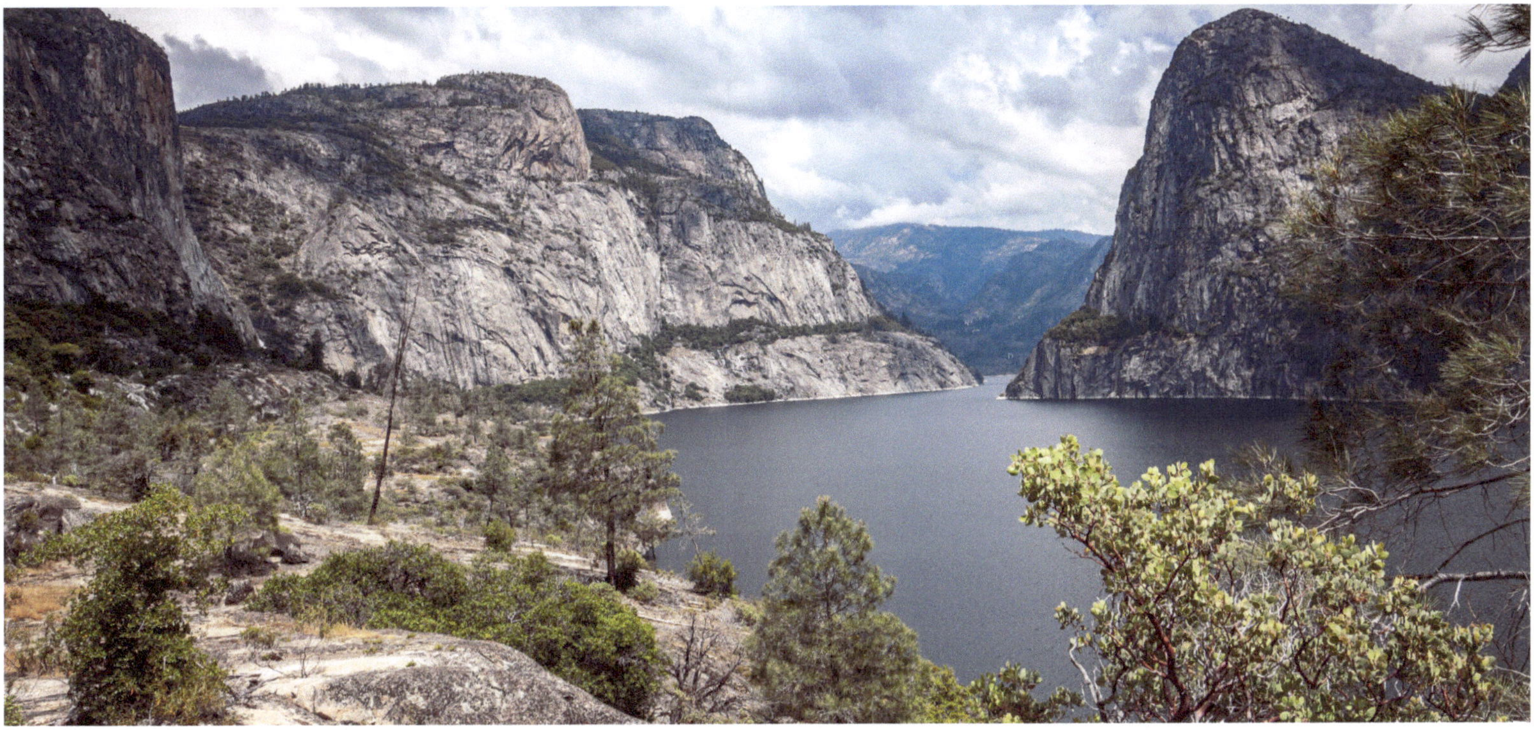

Hetch Hetchy Reservoir (above) and O'Shaughnessy Dam (below)

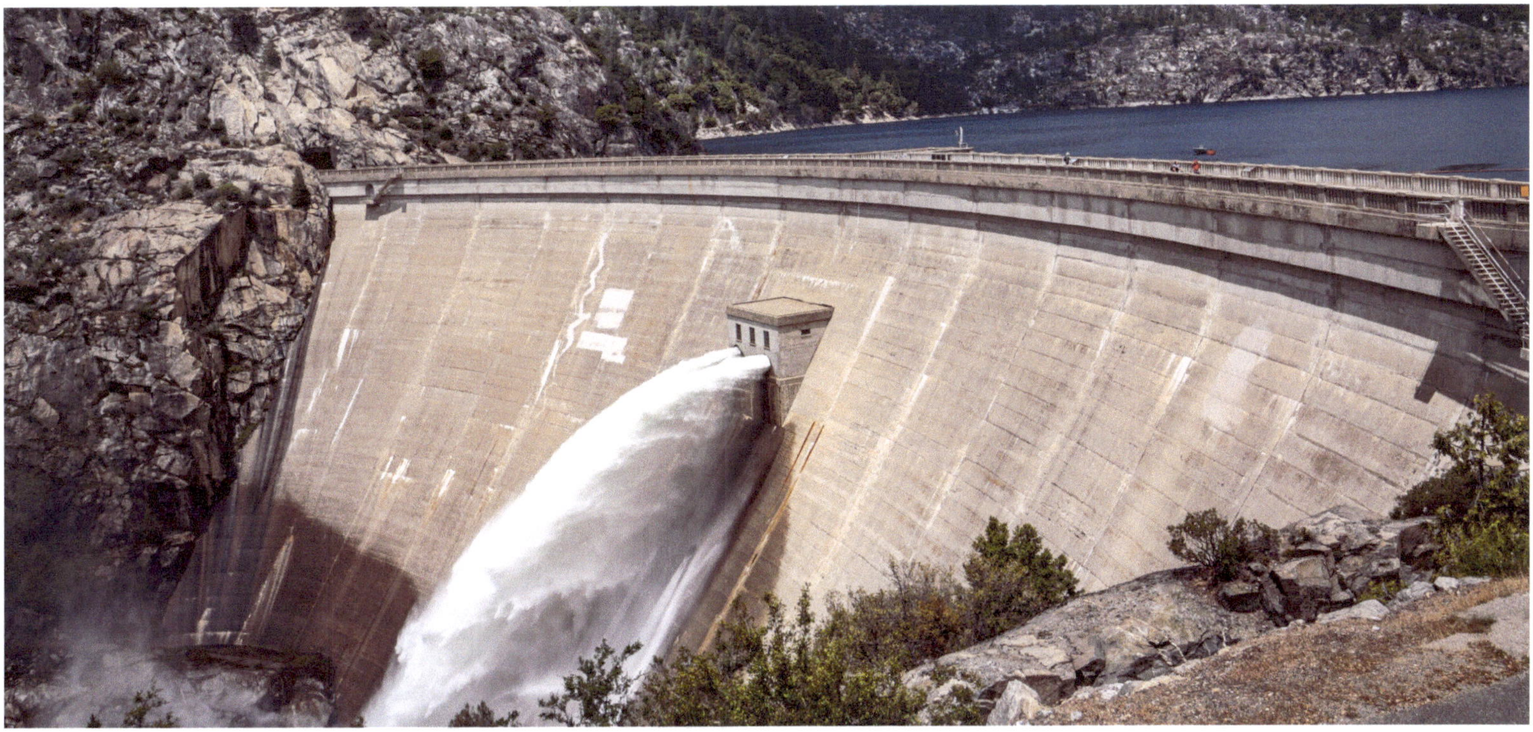

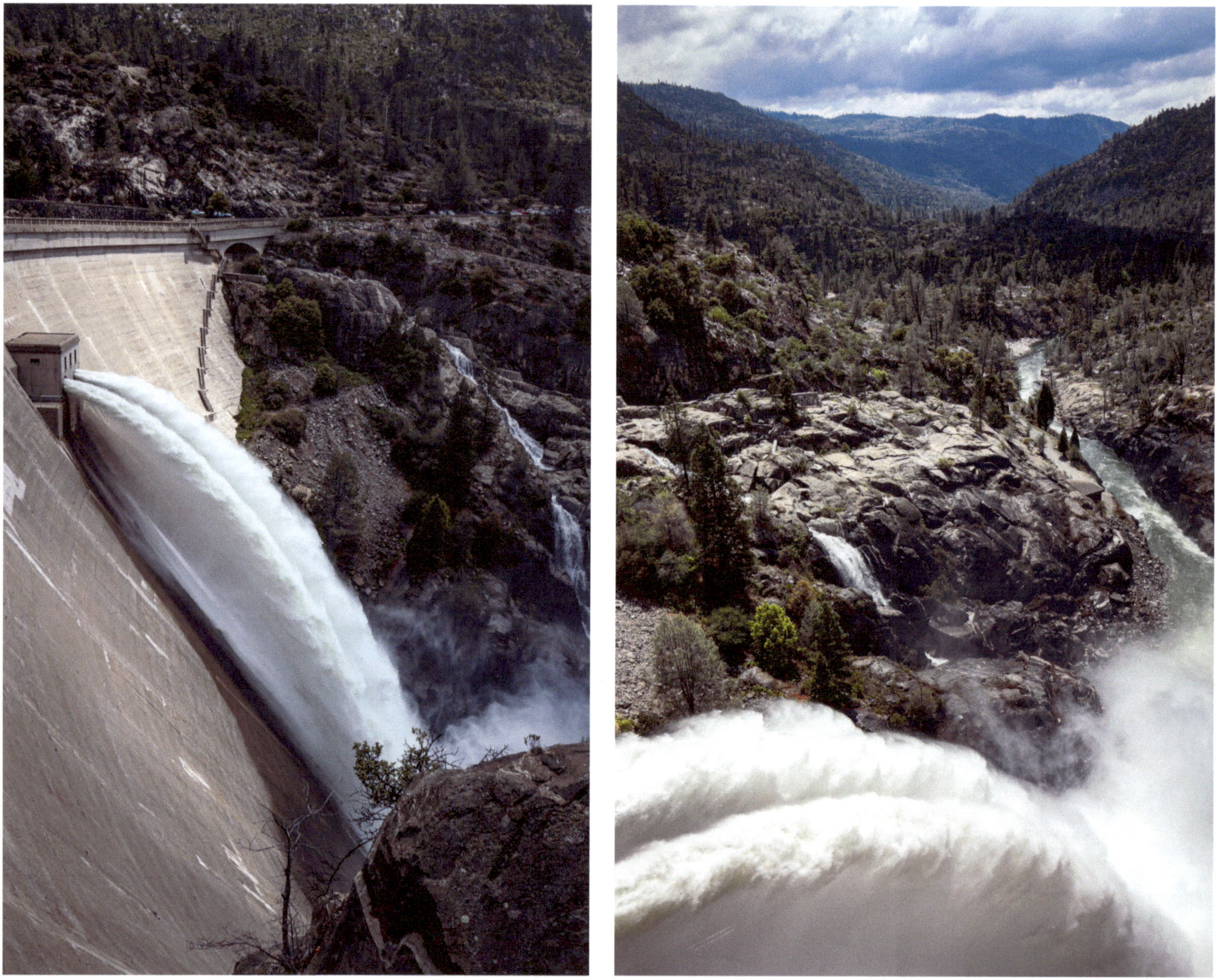

The Hetch Hetchy spillway

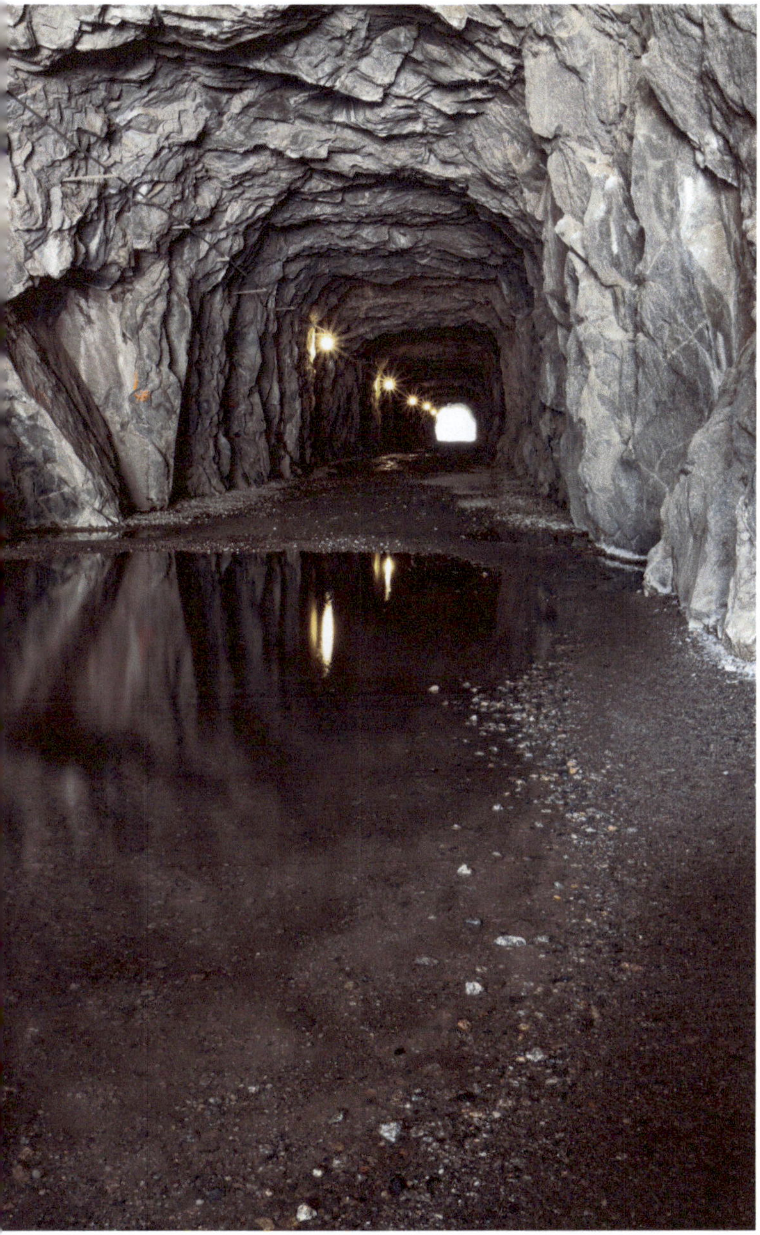

The O'Shaughnessy Dam service tunnel on the
far side of the dam

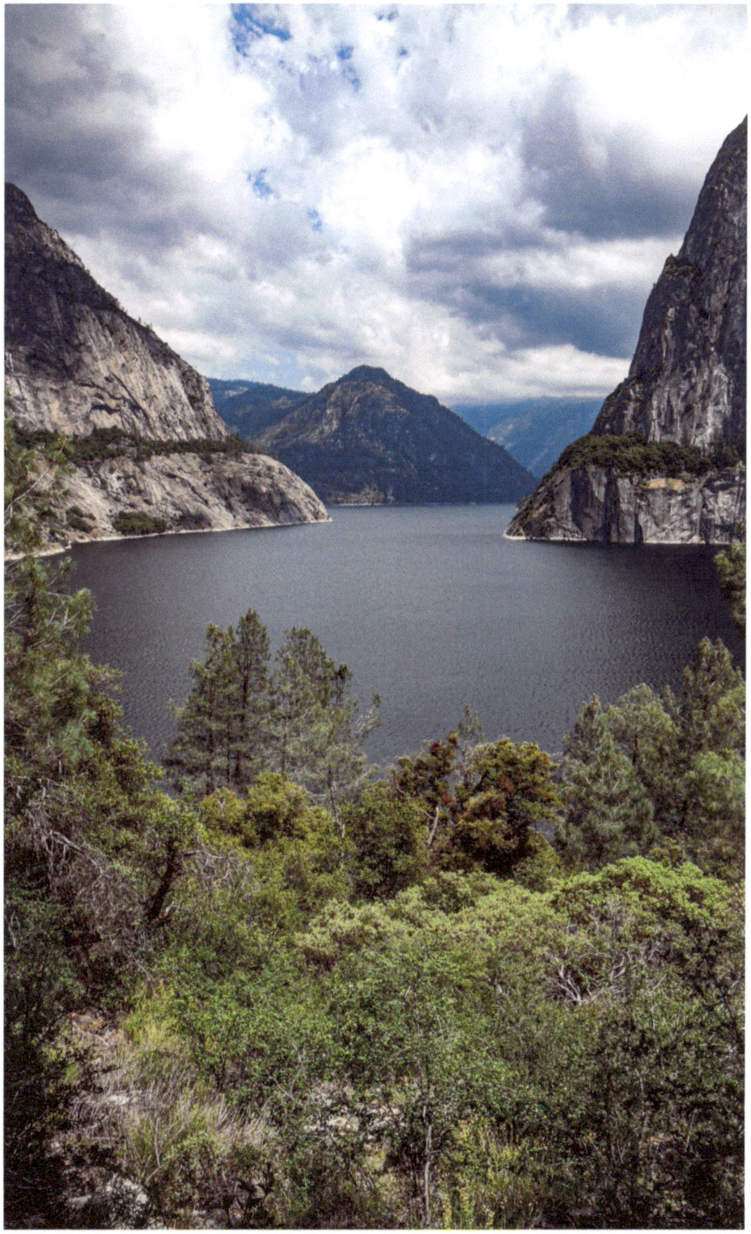

A view of Hetch Hetchy Reservoir after
passing through the tunnel on the trail to
Wapama Falls

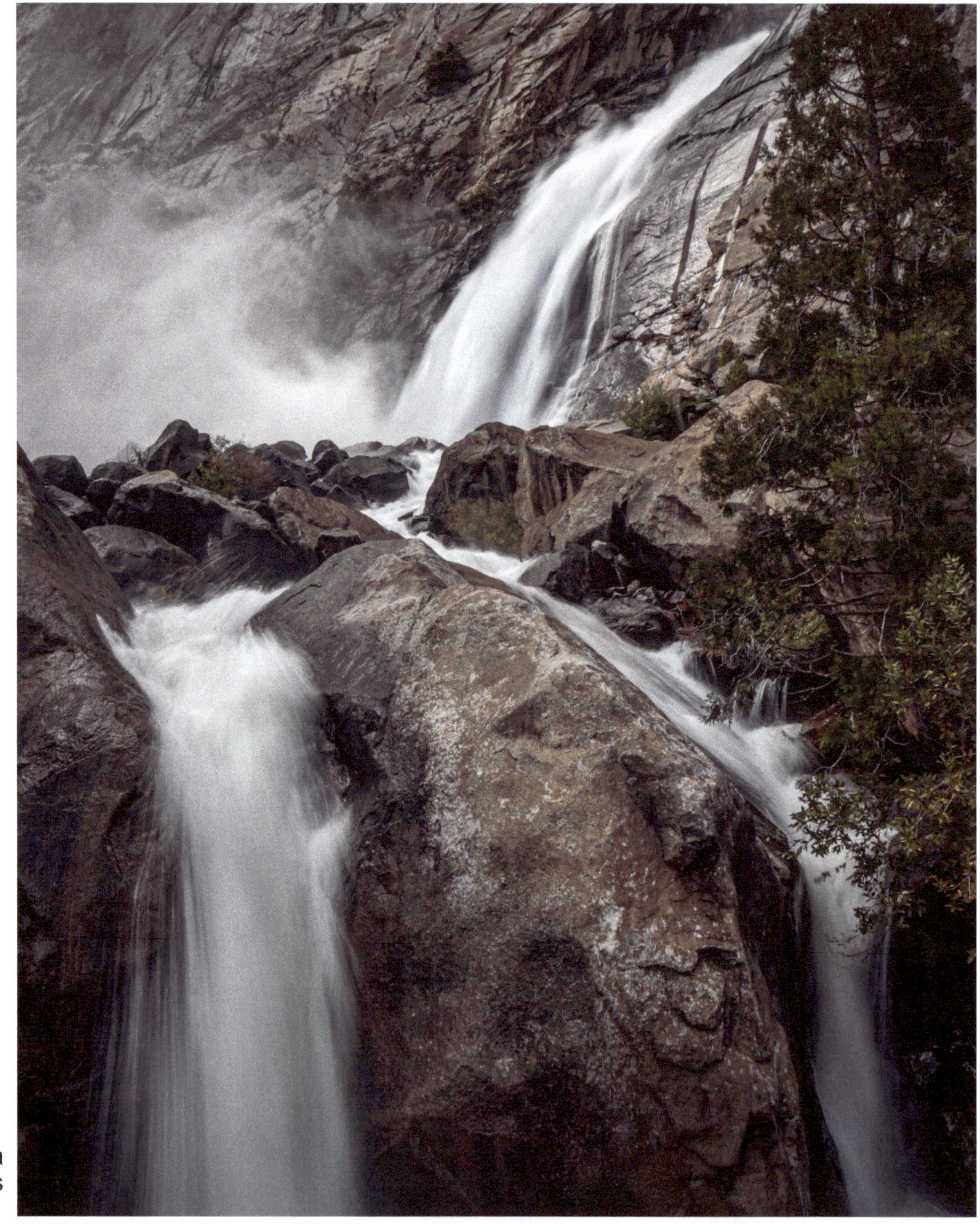

Wapama
Falls

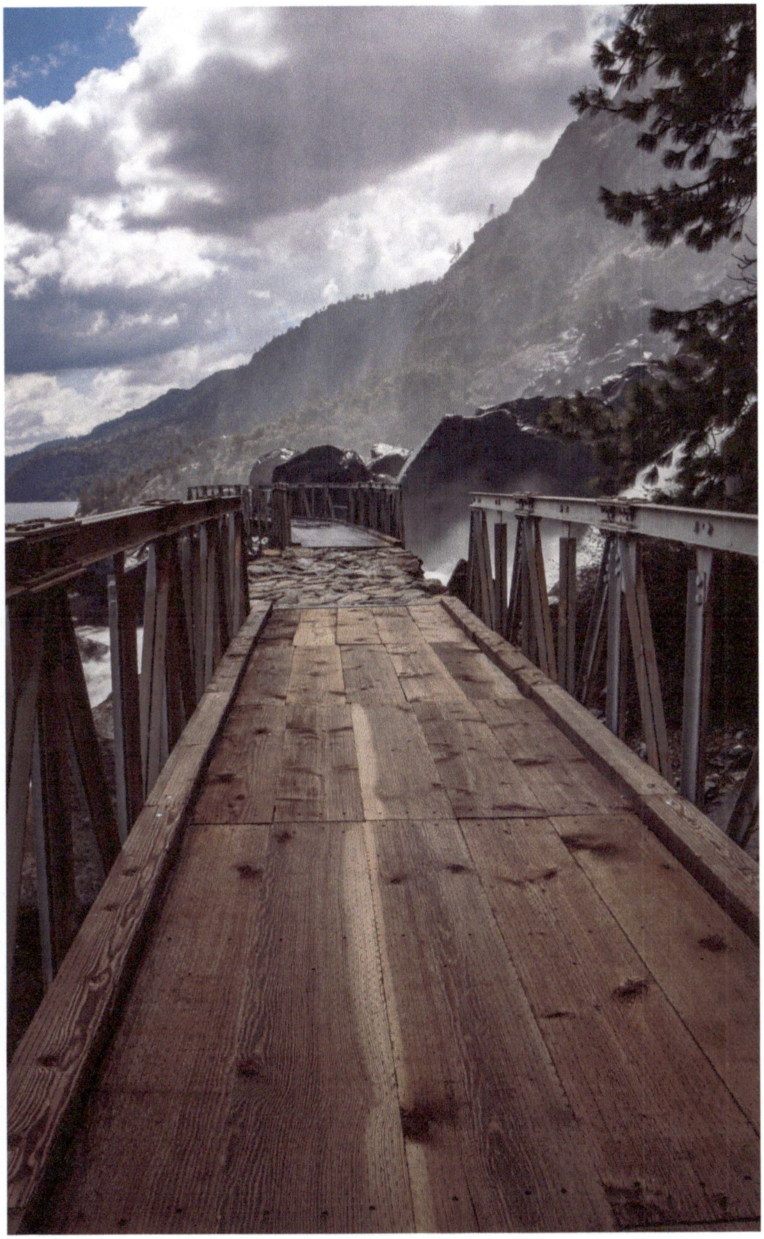

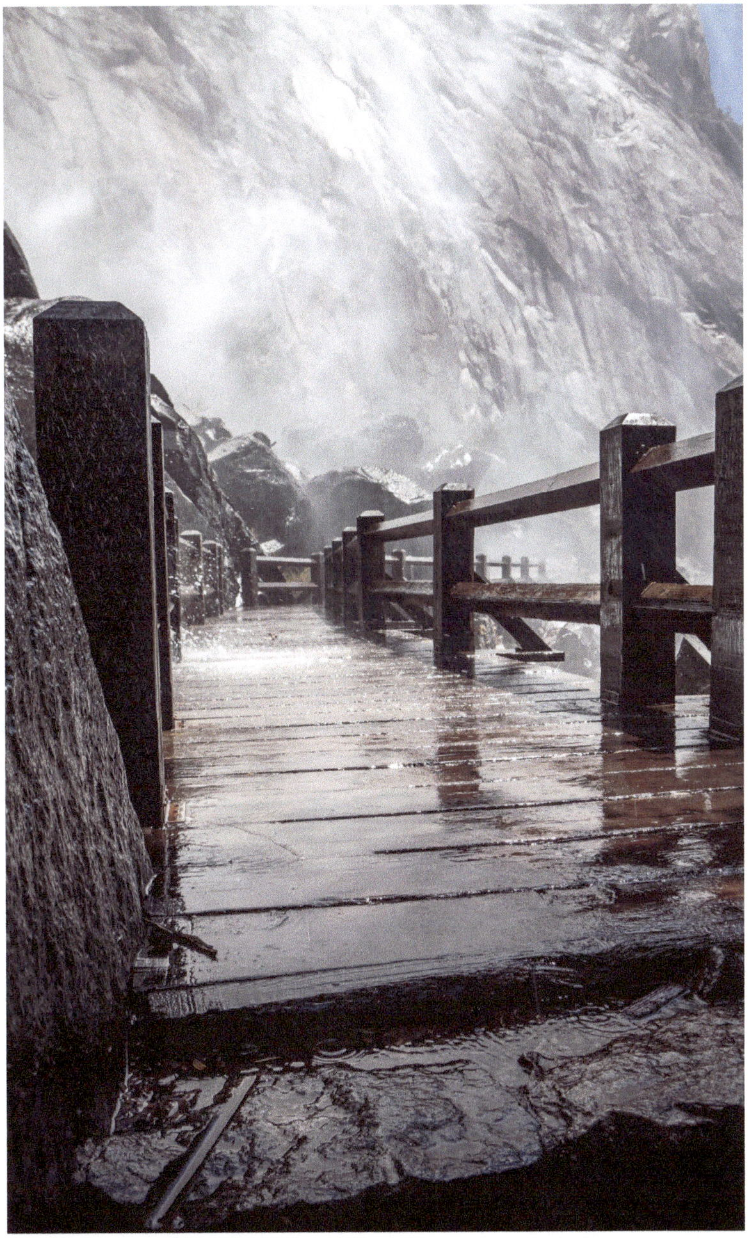

Depending on the season and snowpack, the bridge at the base of Wapama falls can get quite wet

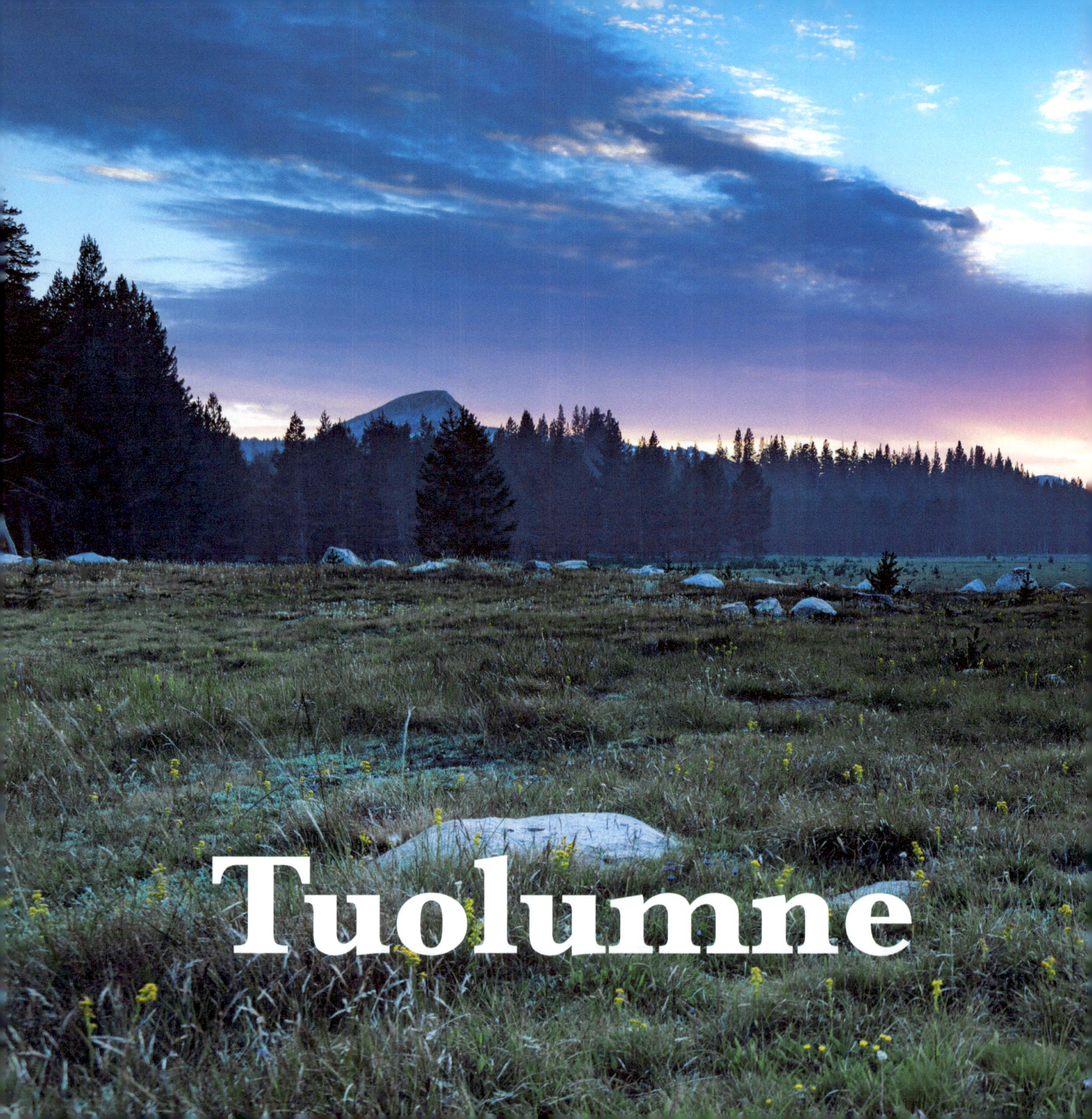
Tuolumne

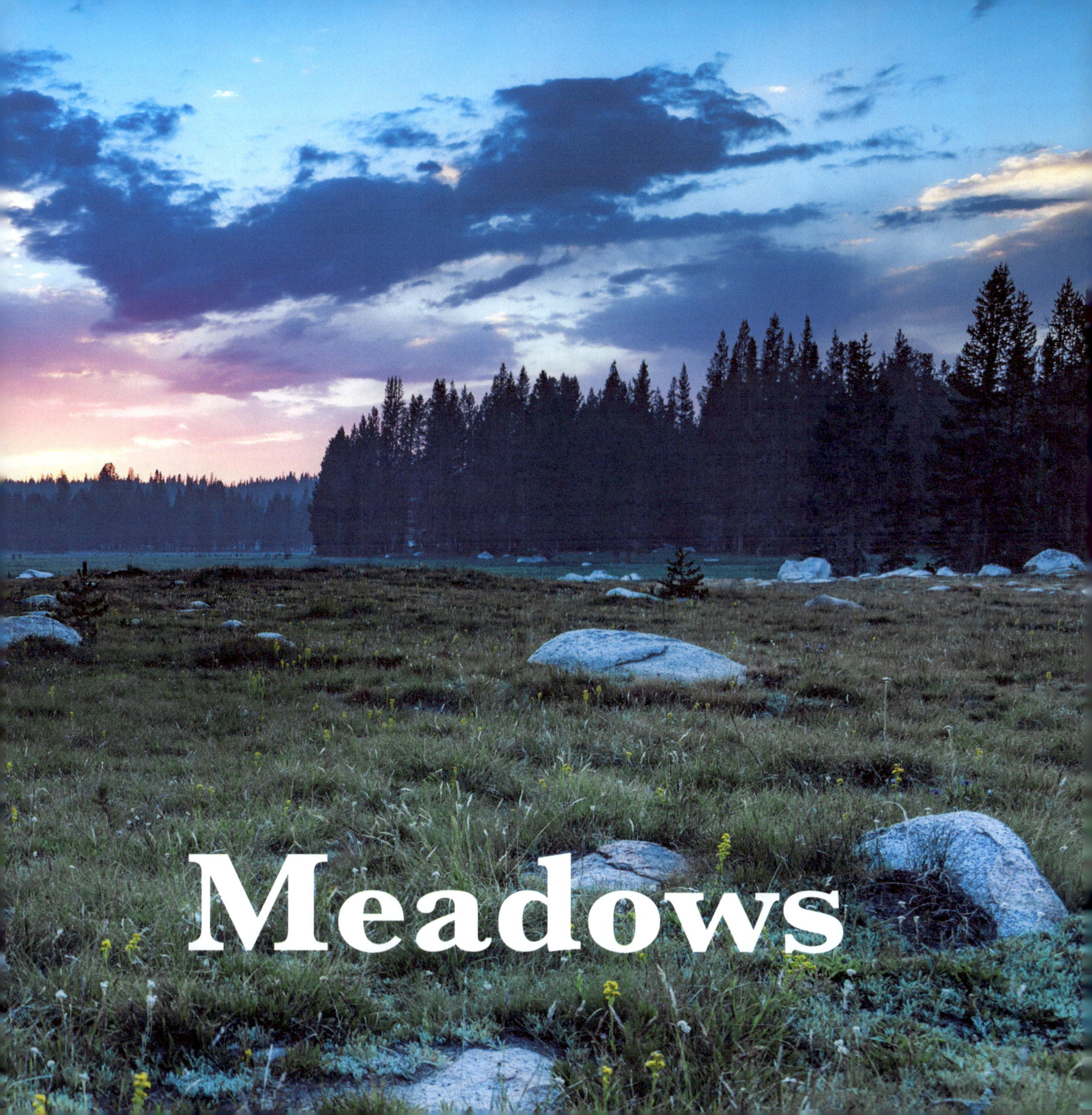
Meadows

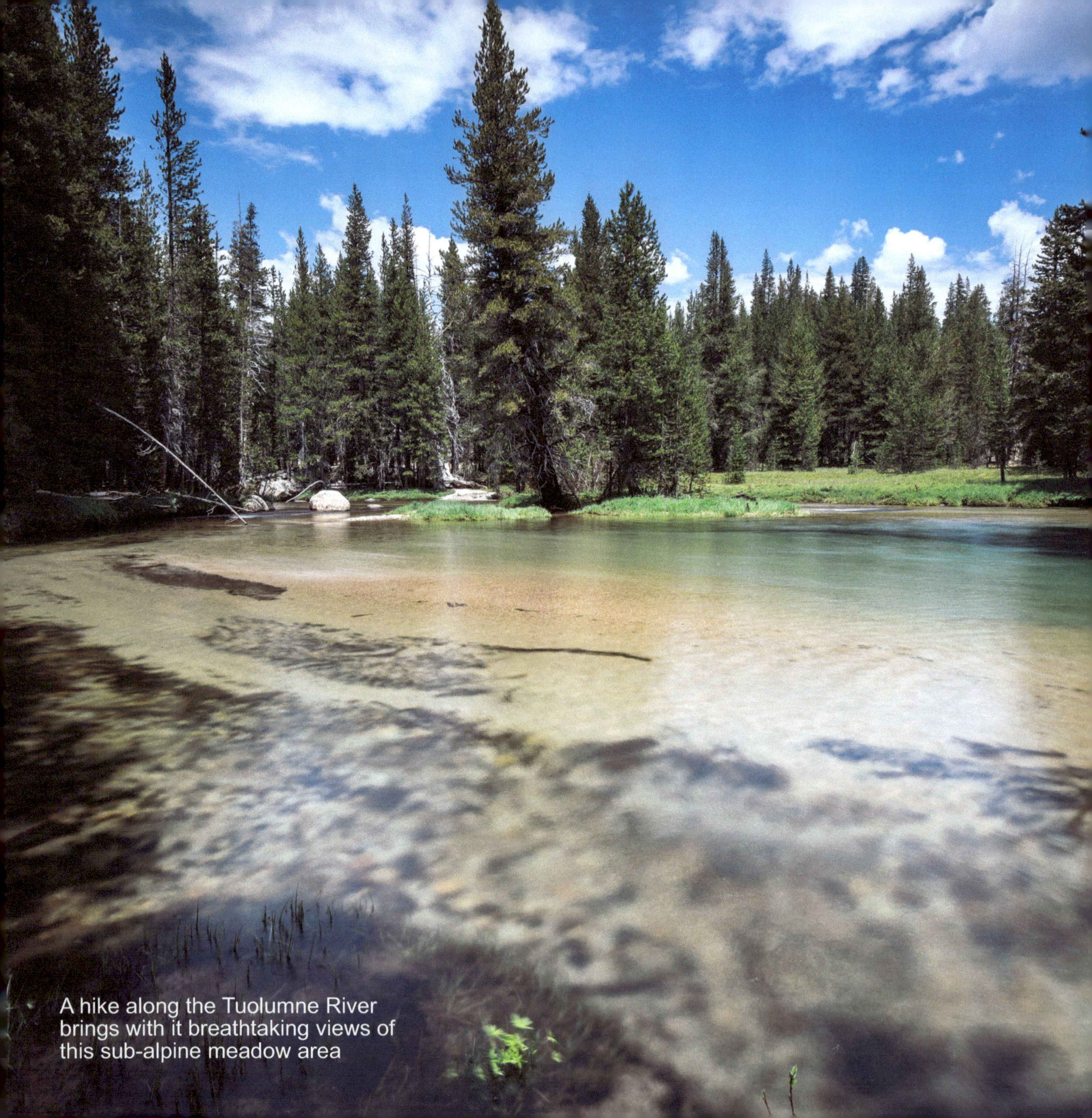

A hike along the Tuolumne River
brings with it breathtaking views of
this sub-alpine meadow area

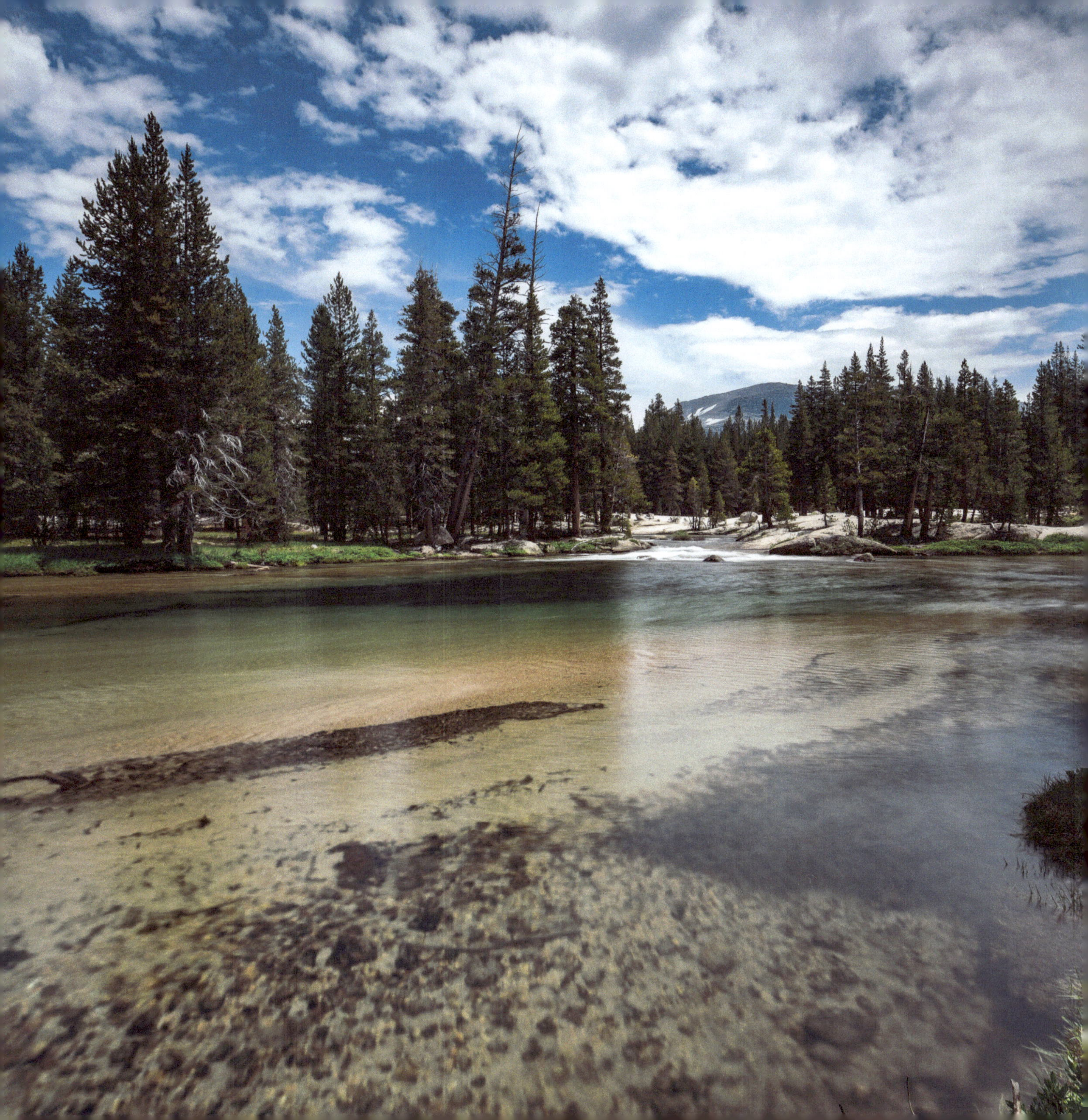

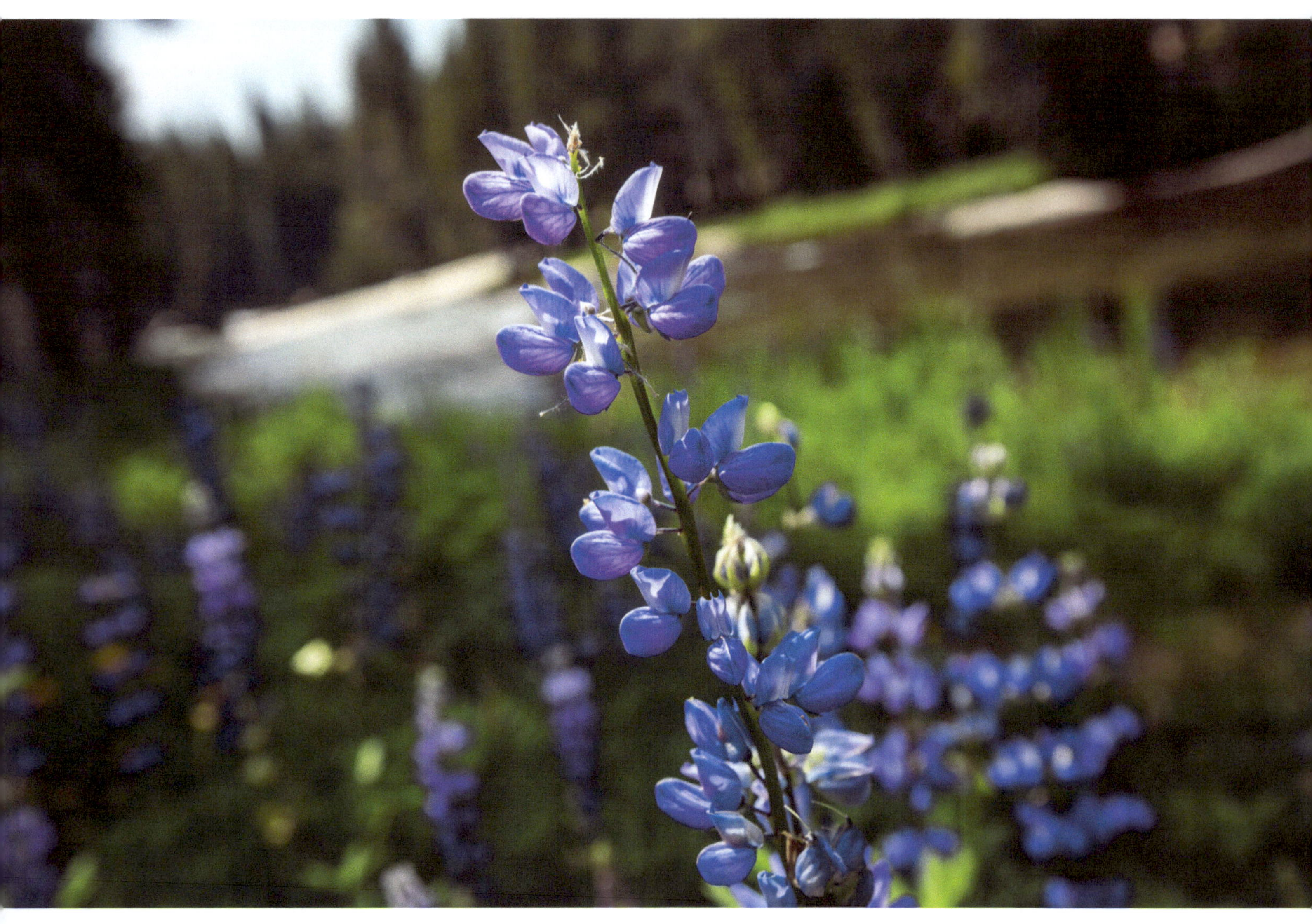

Lupins along the Tuolumne River

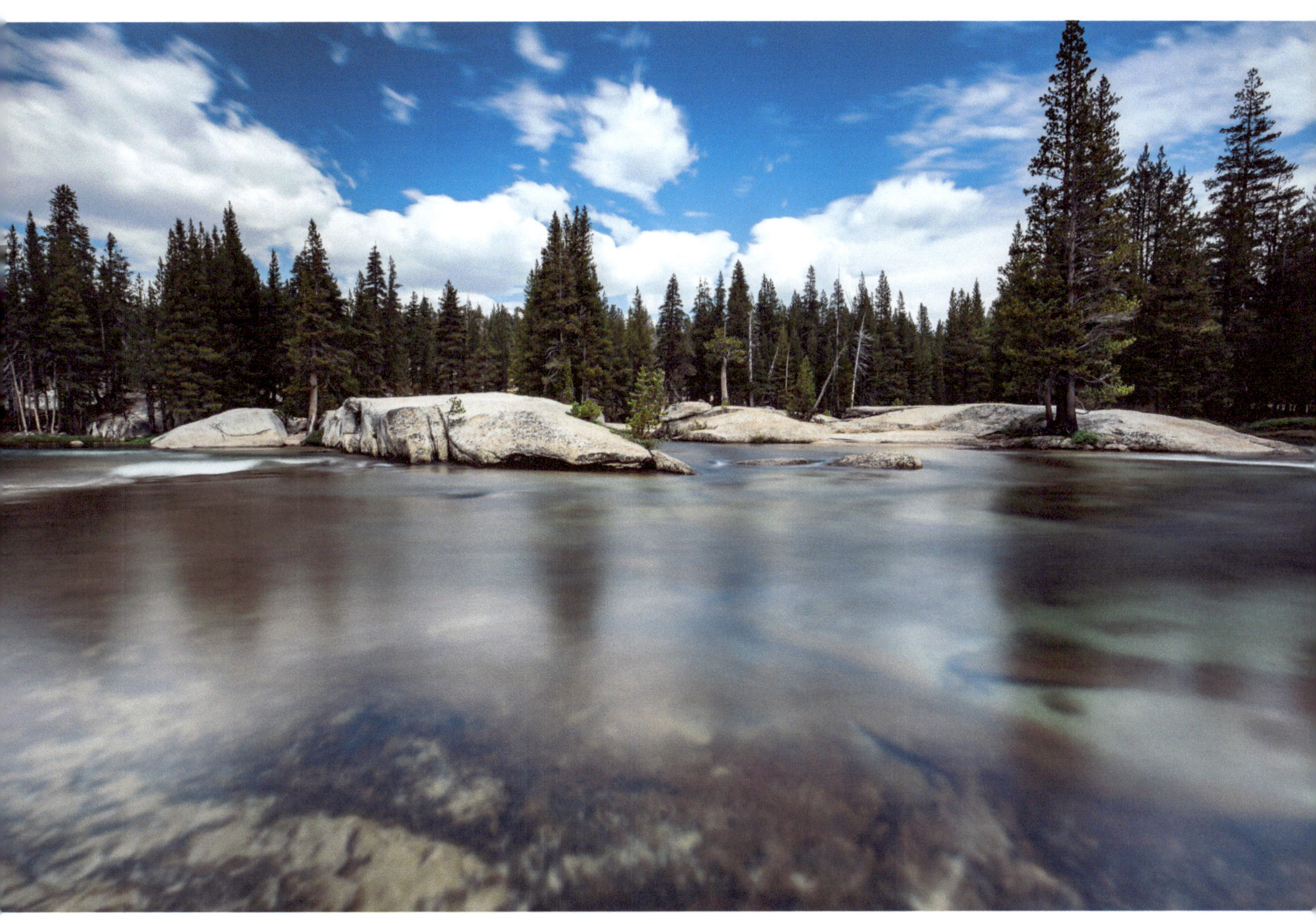

Pools form in sections of the Tuolumne River in the upper meadows

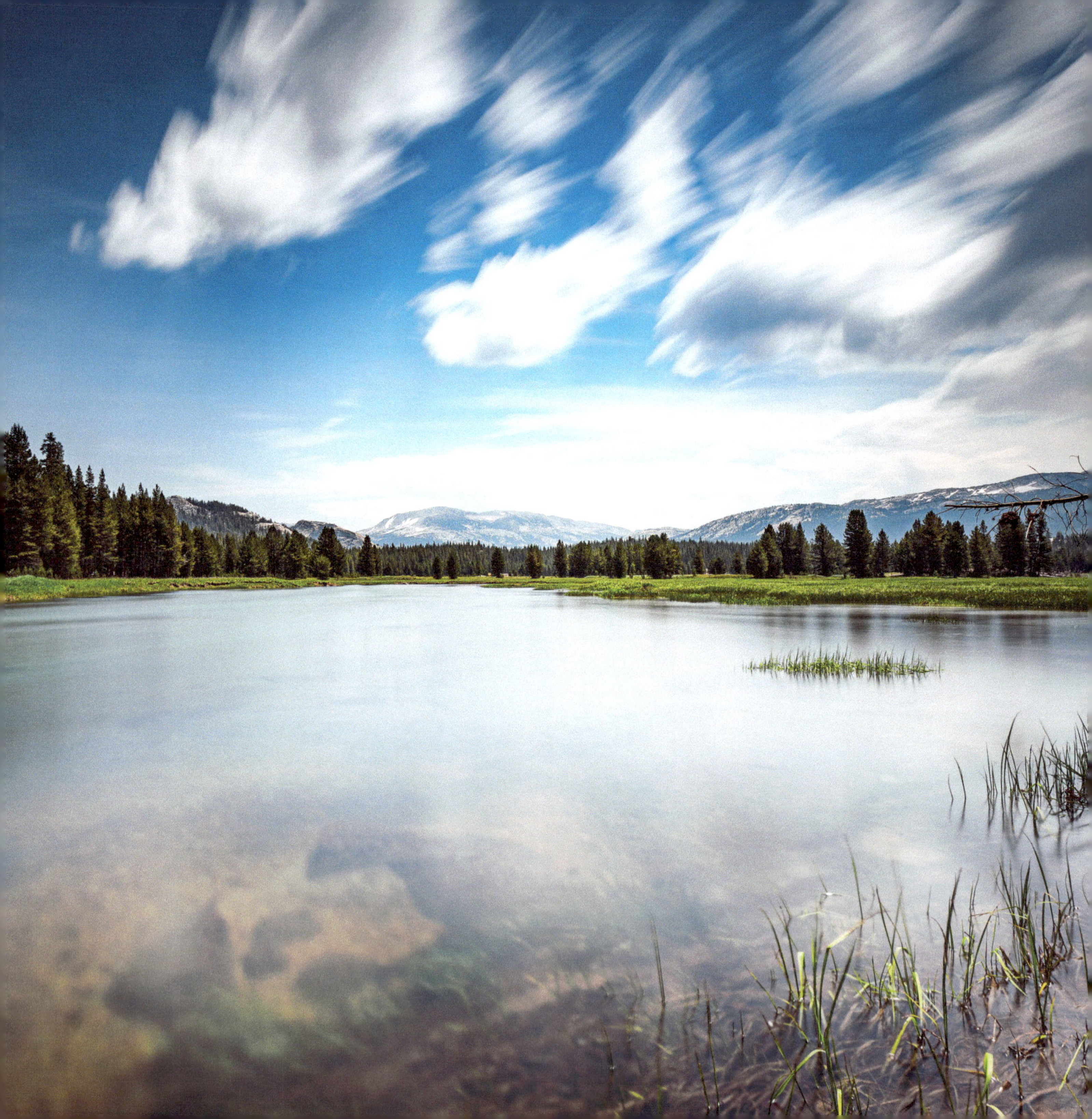

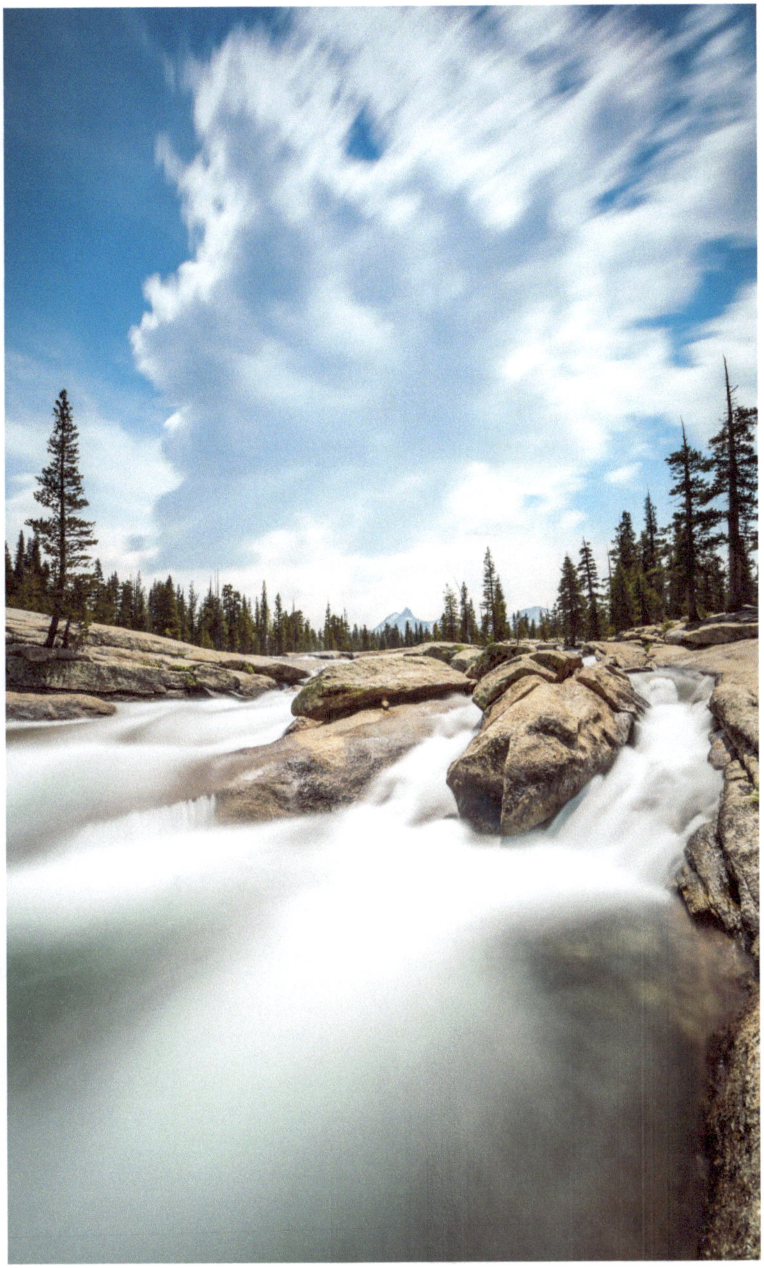

Summer thunderstorms move in across the meadows and the lower cascades of the Tuolumne River

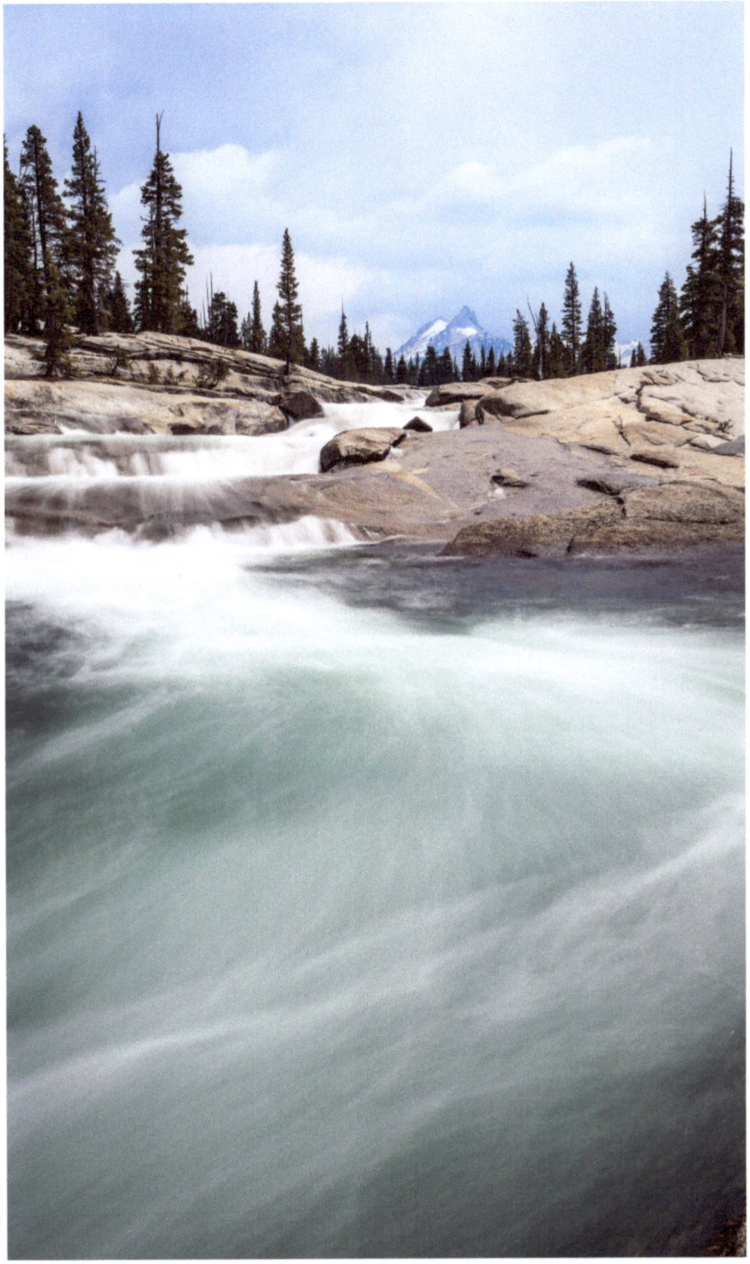

The Tuolumne River winds down areas of exposed granite and eventually makes it's way into Hetch Hetchy Reservoir

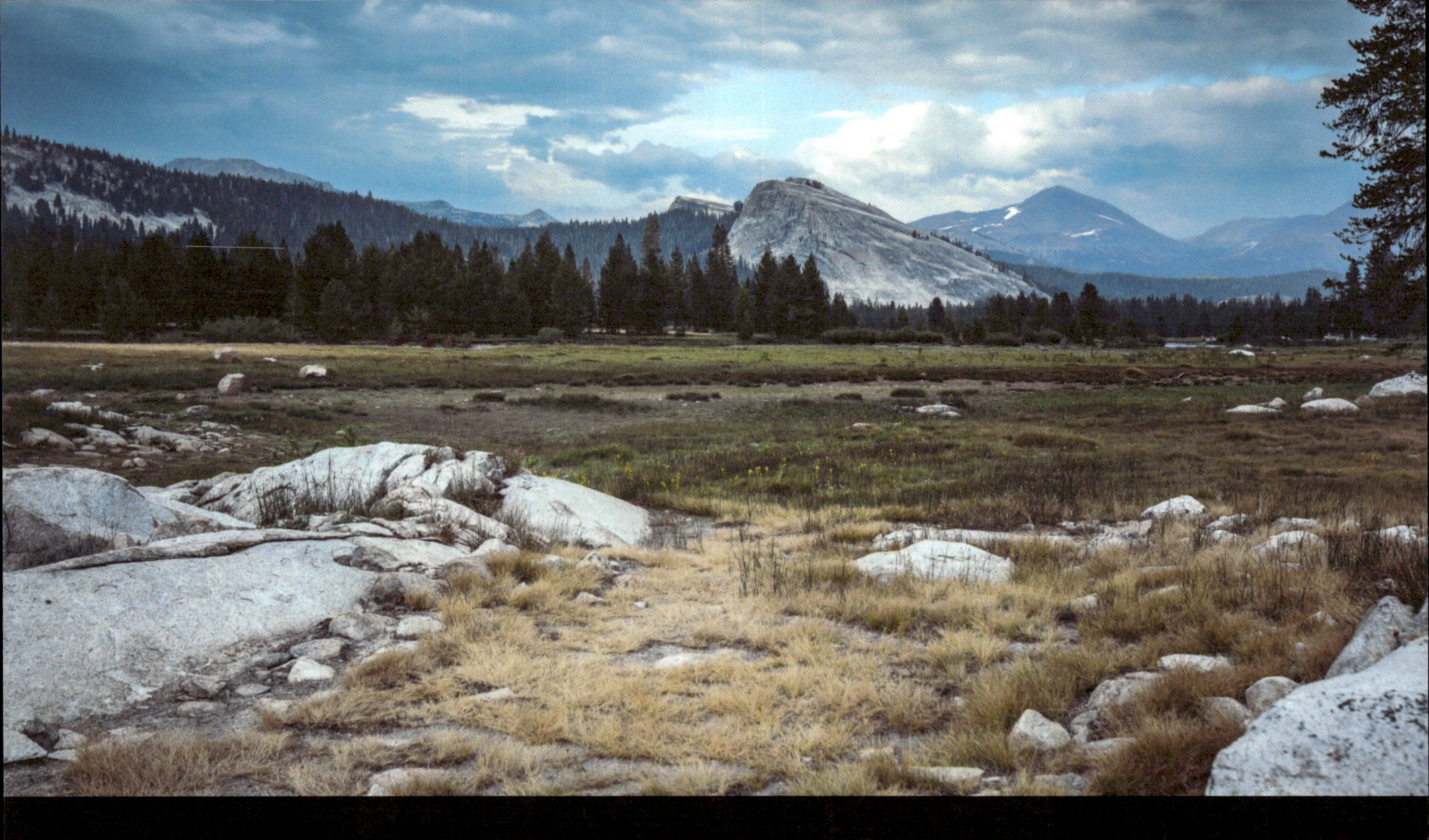

Tuolumne Meadows as summer storms move over the mountains in the evening hours

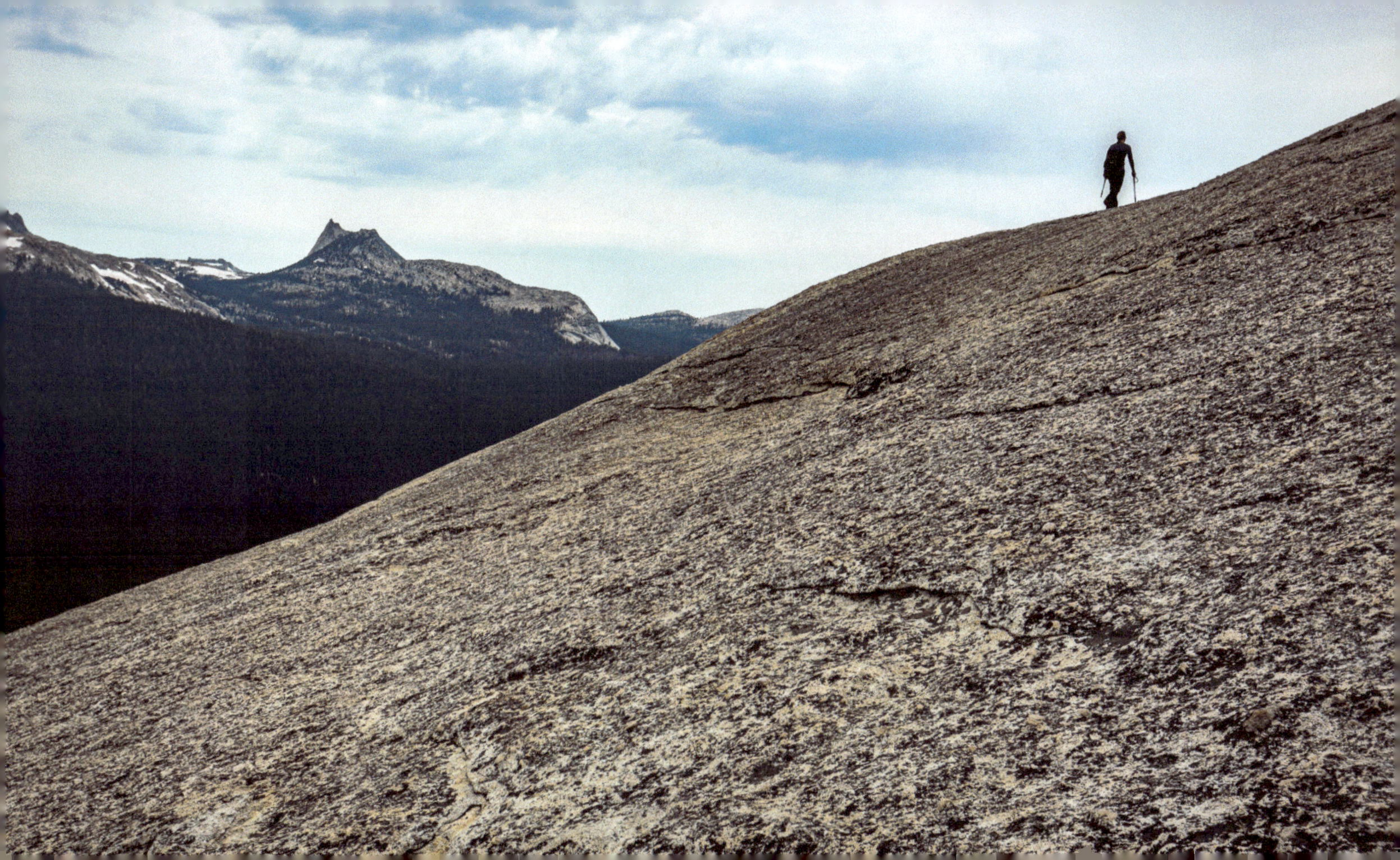

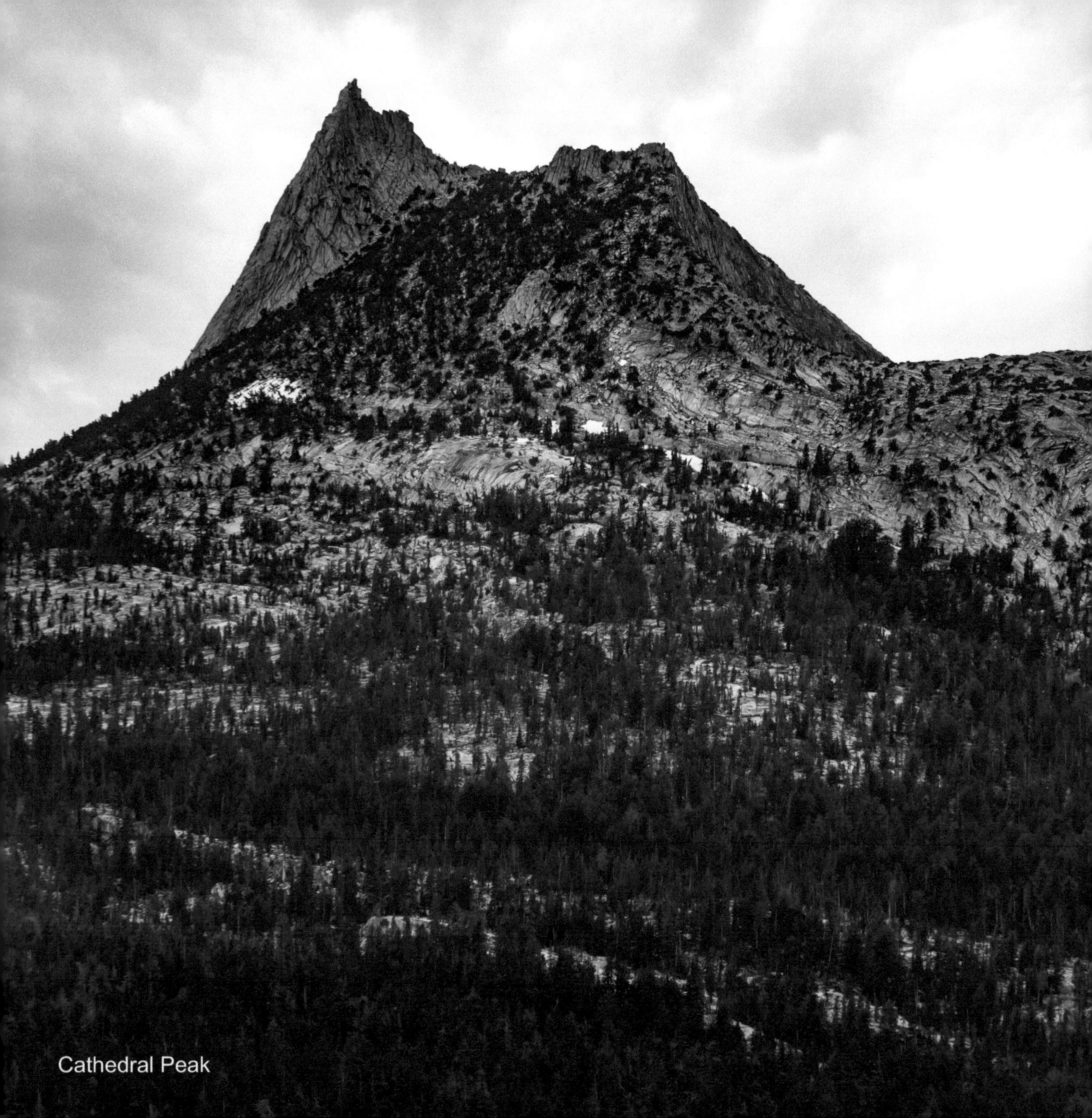
Cathedral Peak

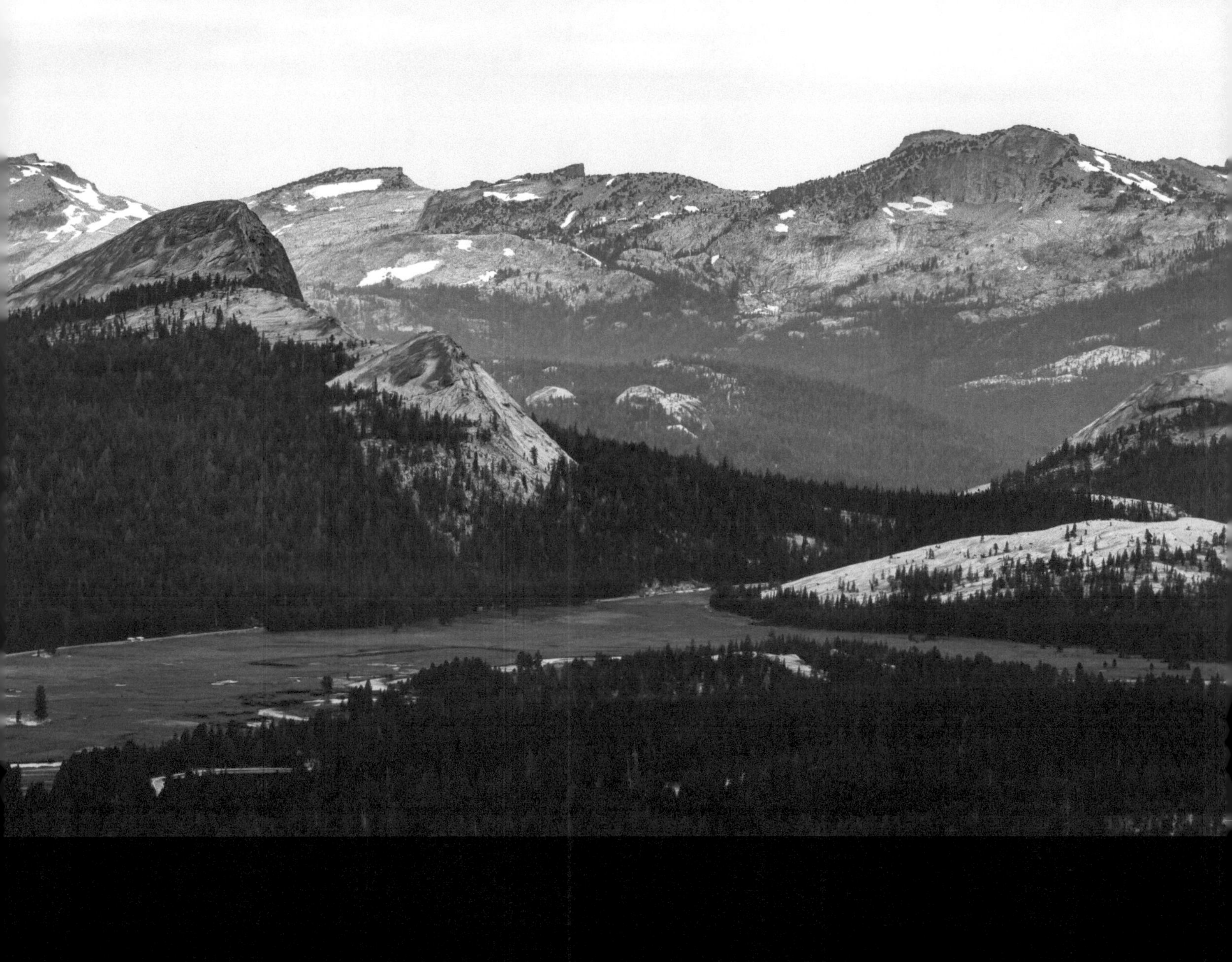

Fairview Dome, Marmot Dome and Pothole Dome

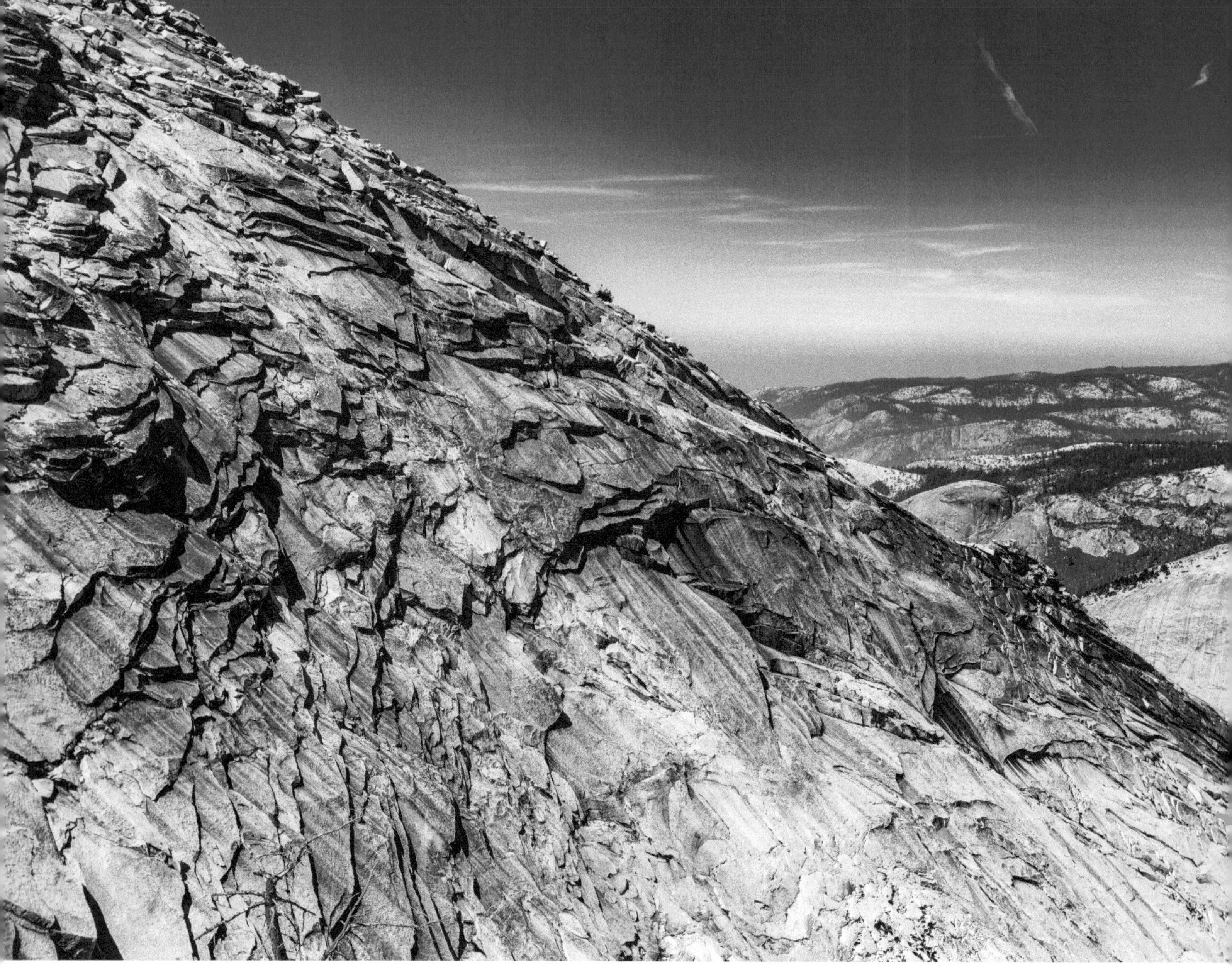

Clouds Rest

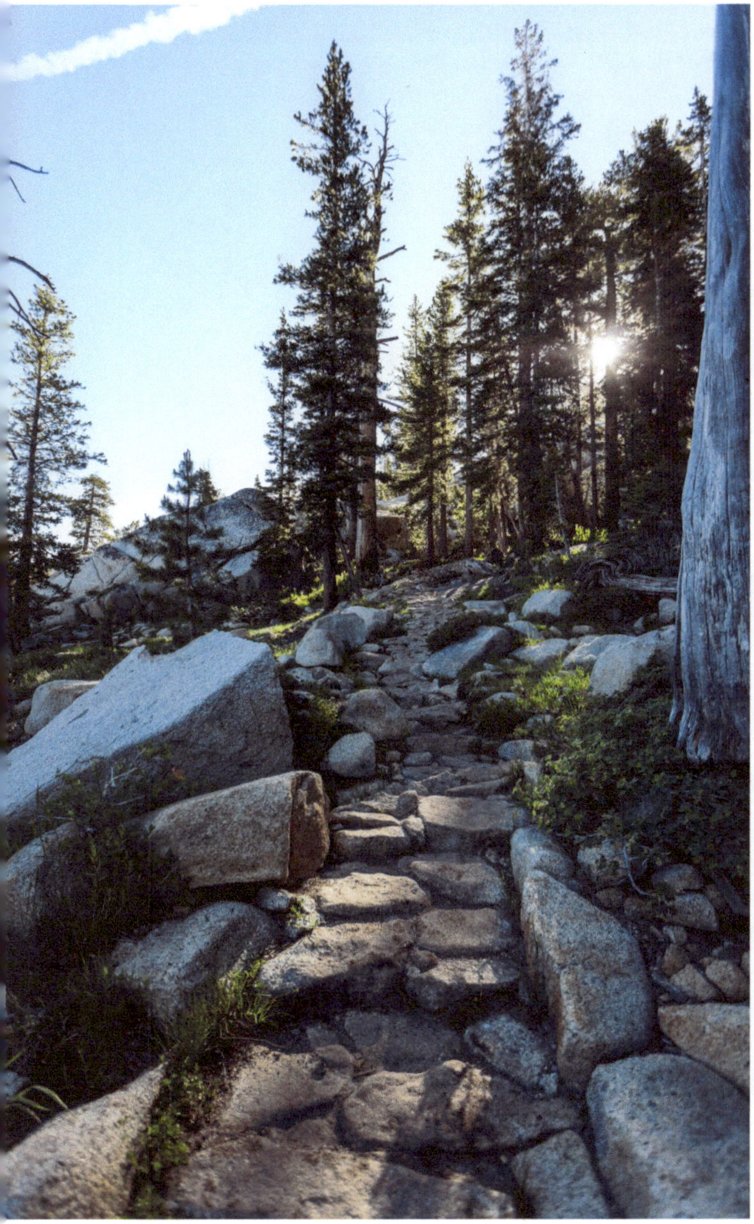

The Clouds Rest Trail

Clouds Rest is a fantastic alternative to the
overcrowded Half Dome hike

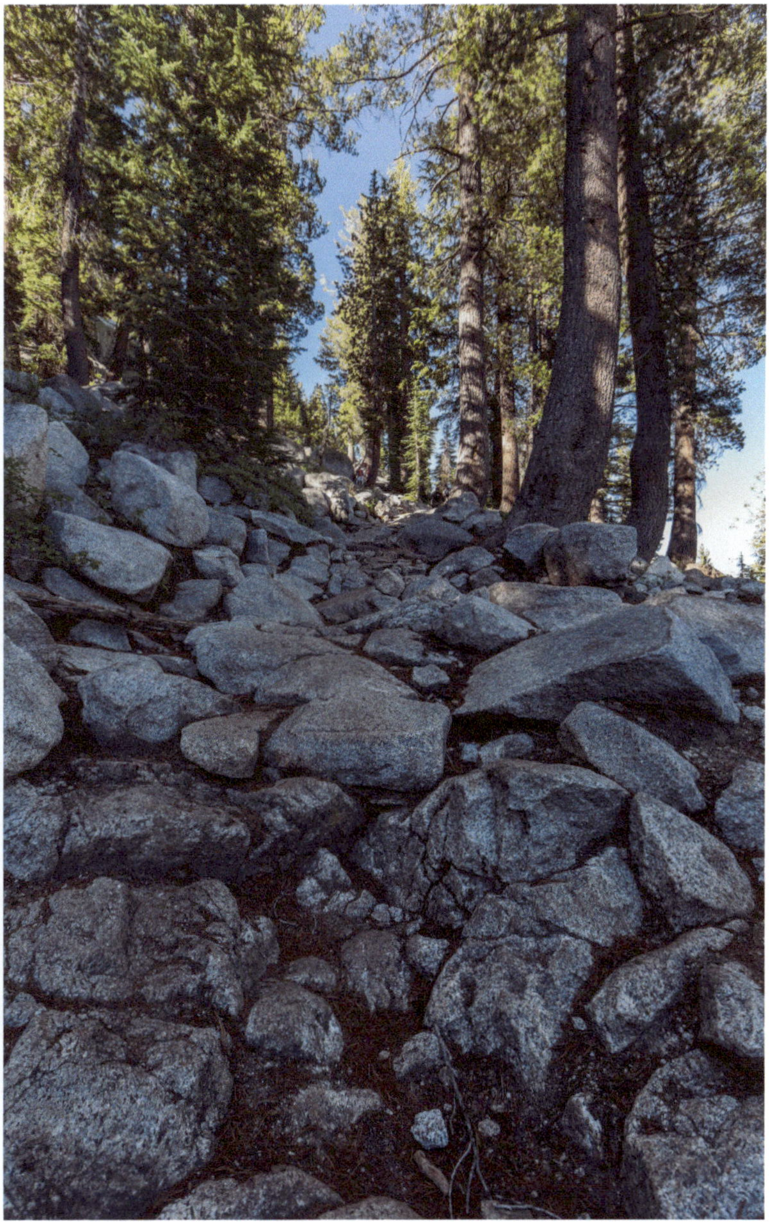

The trail to Clouds Rest on the first ascent
looks more like a boulder scramble than a trail

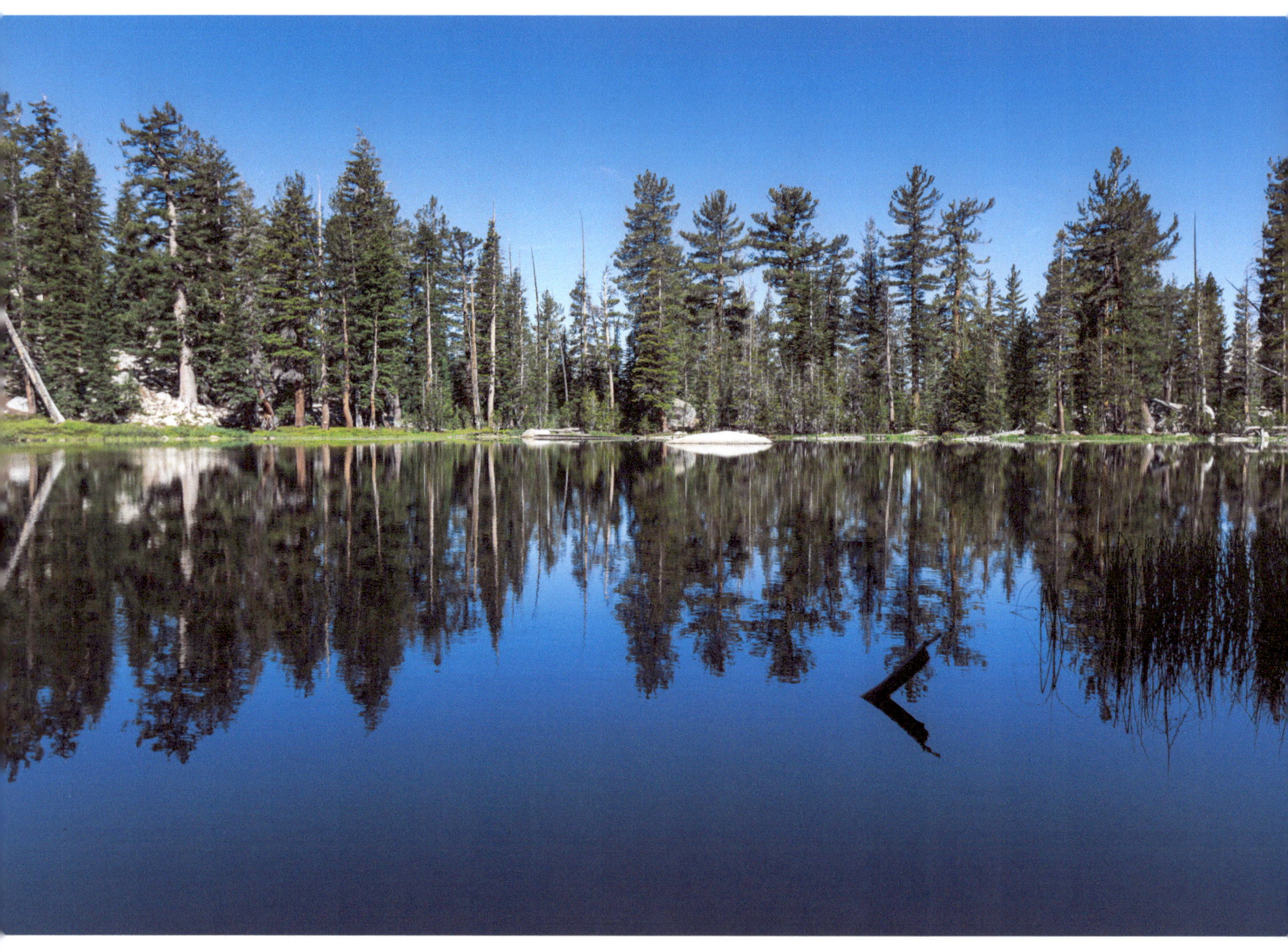

Reflections in a pond along the Clouds Rest Trail

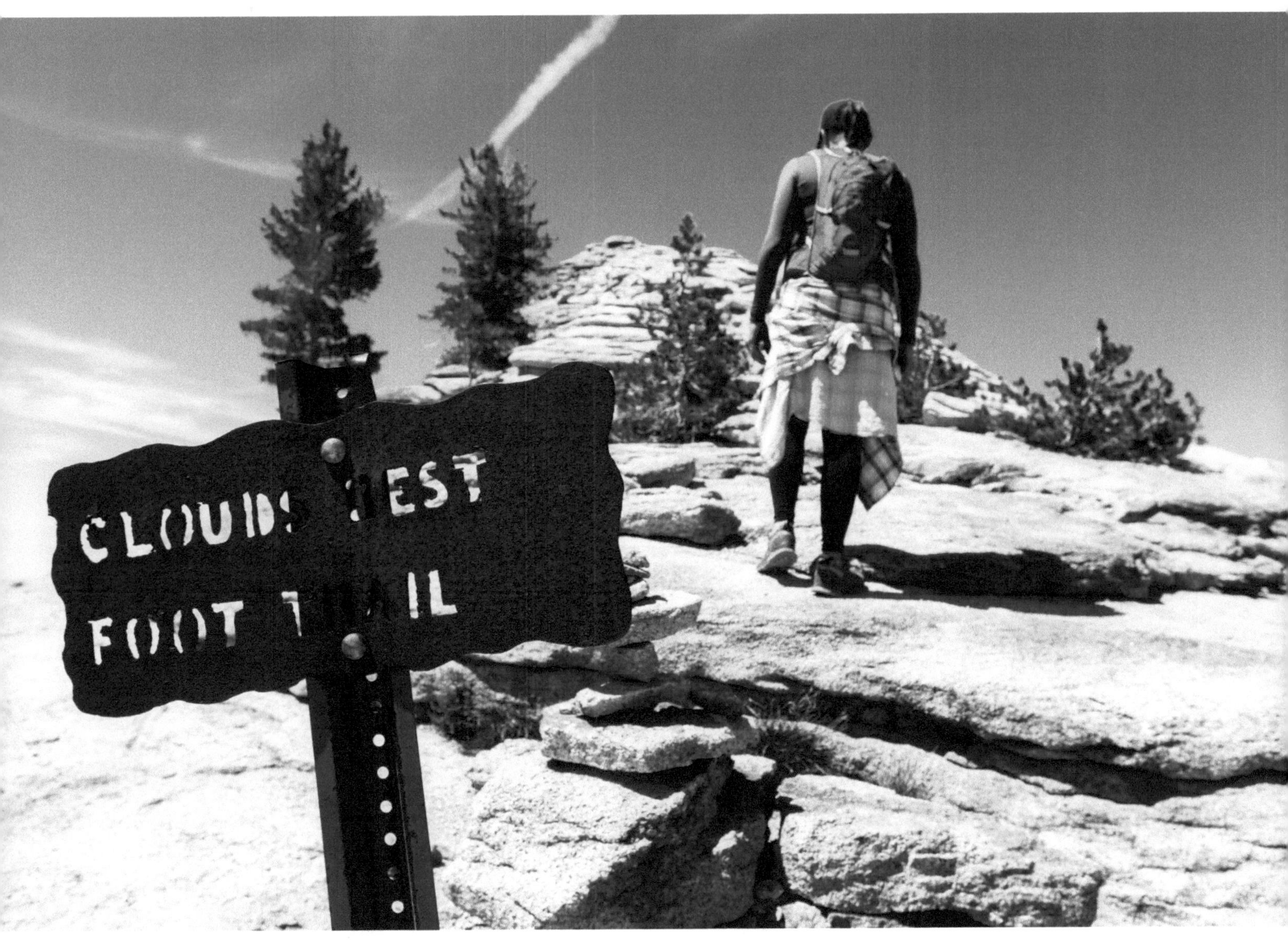

Summiting Clouds Rest

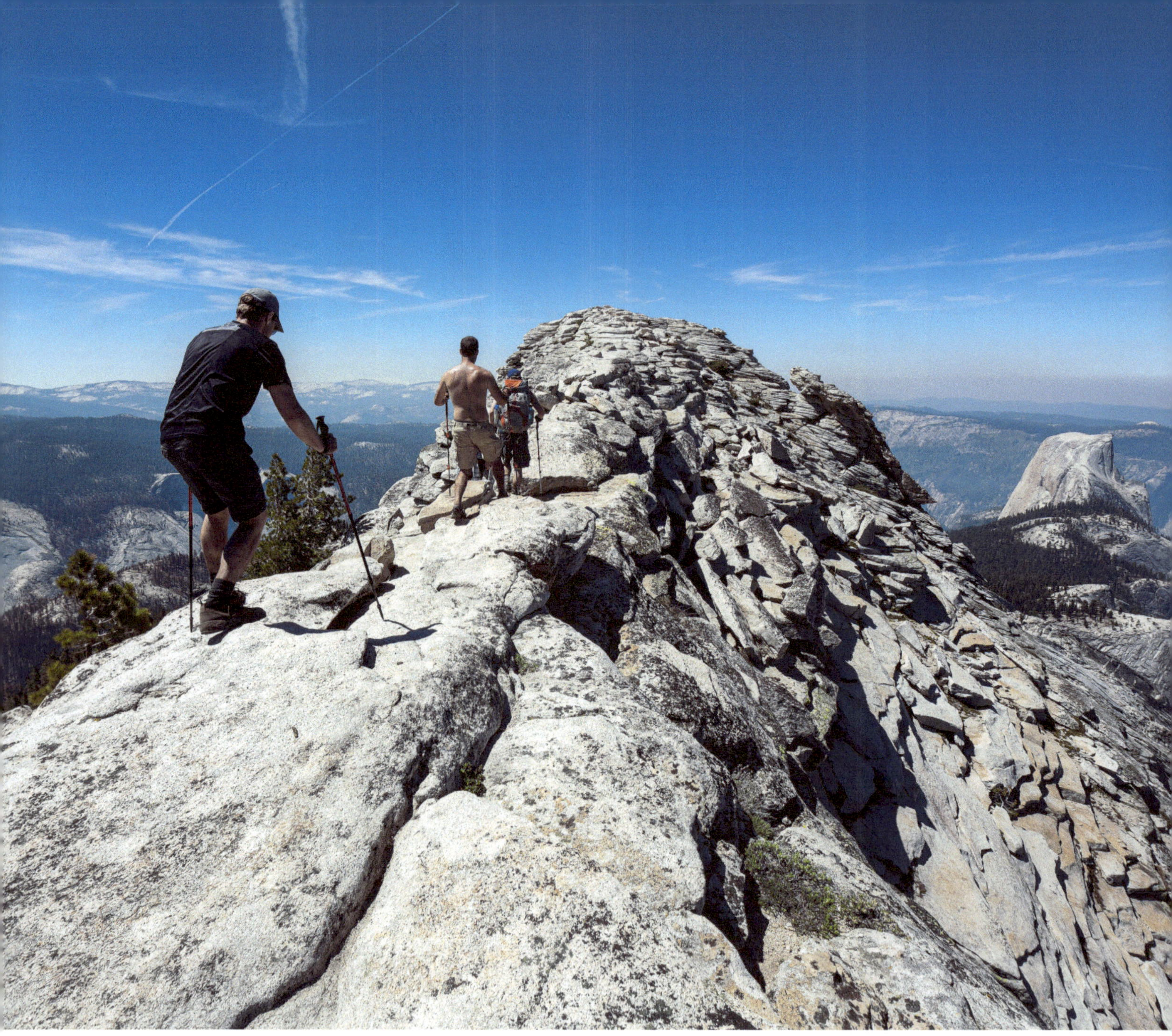

The Spine on the way to the summit of Clouds Rest

Half Dome and Yosemite Valley are in the background

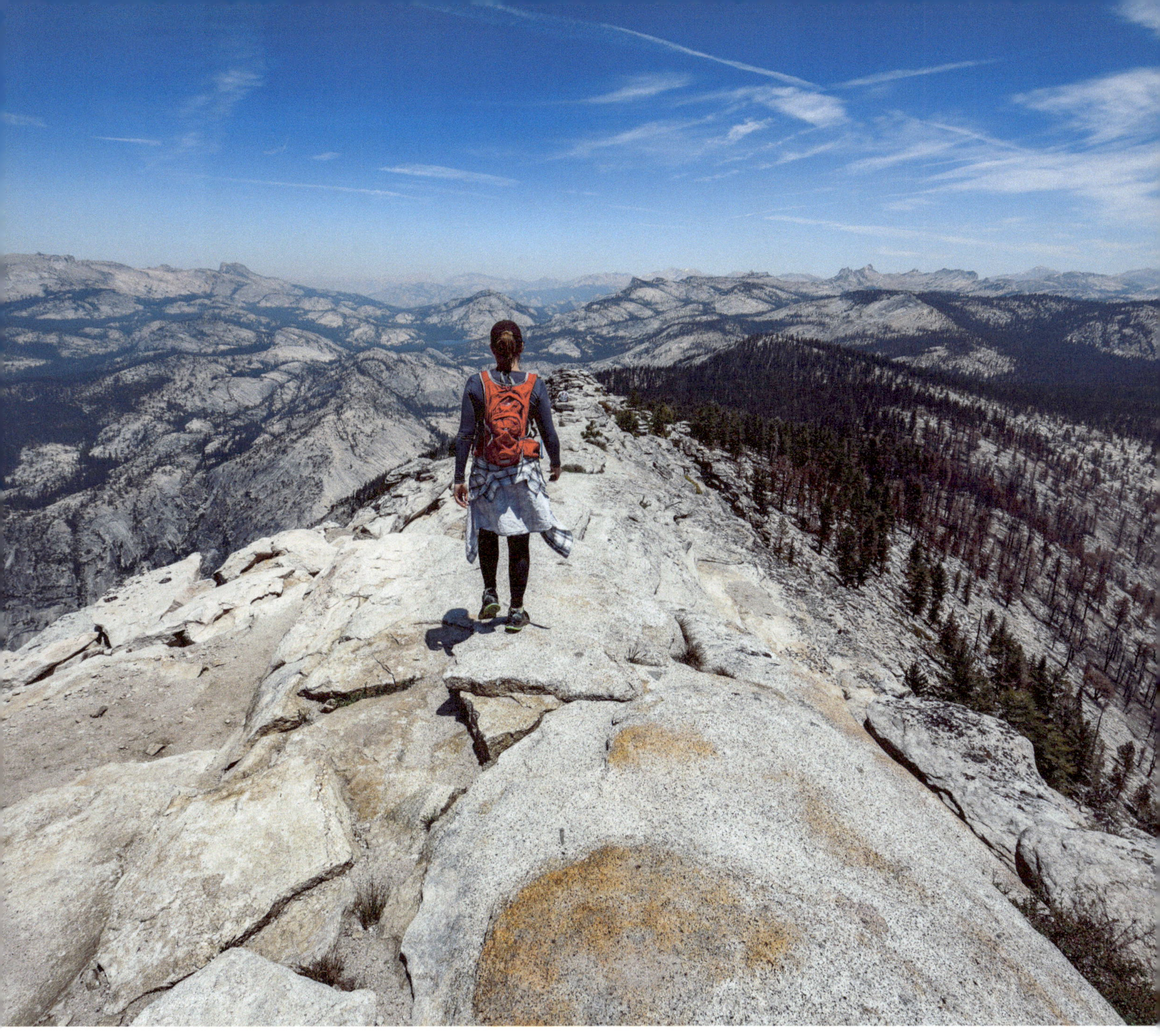

The spine is not for the faint of heart, but it offers some incredible views

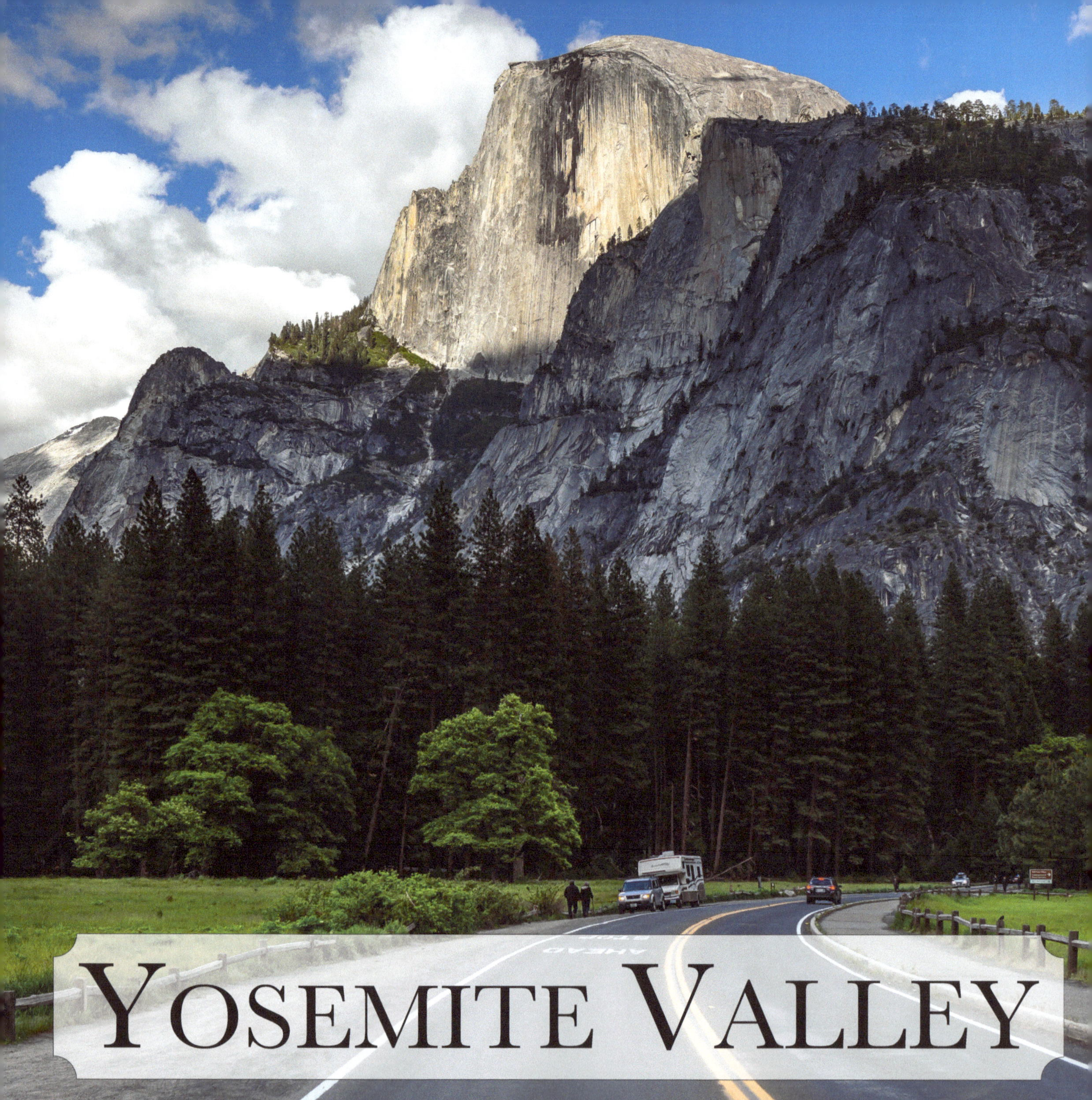

YOSEMITE VALLEY

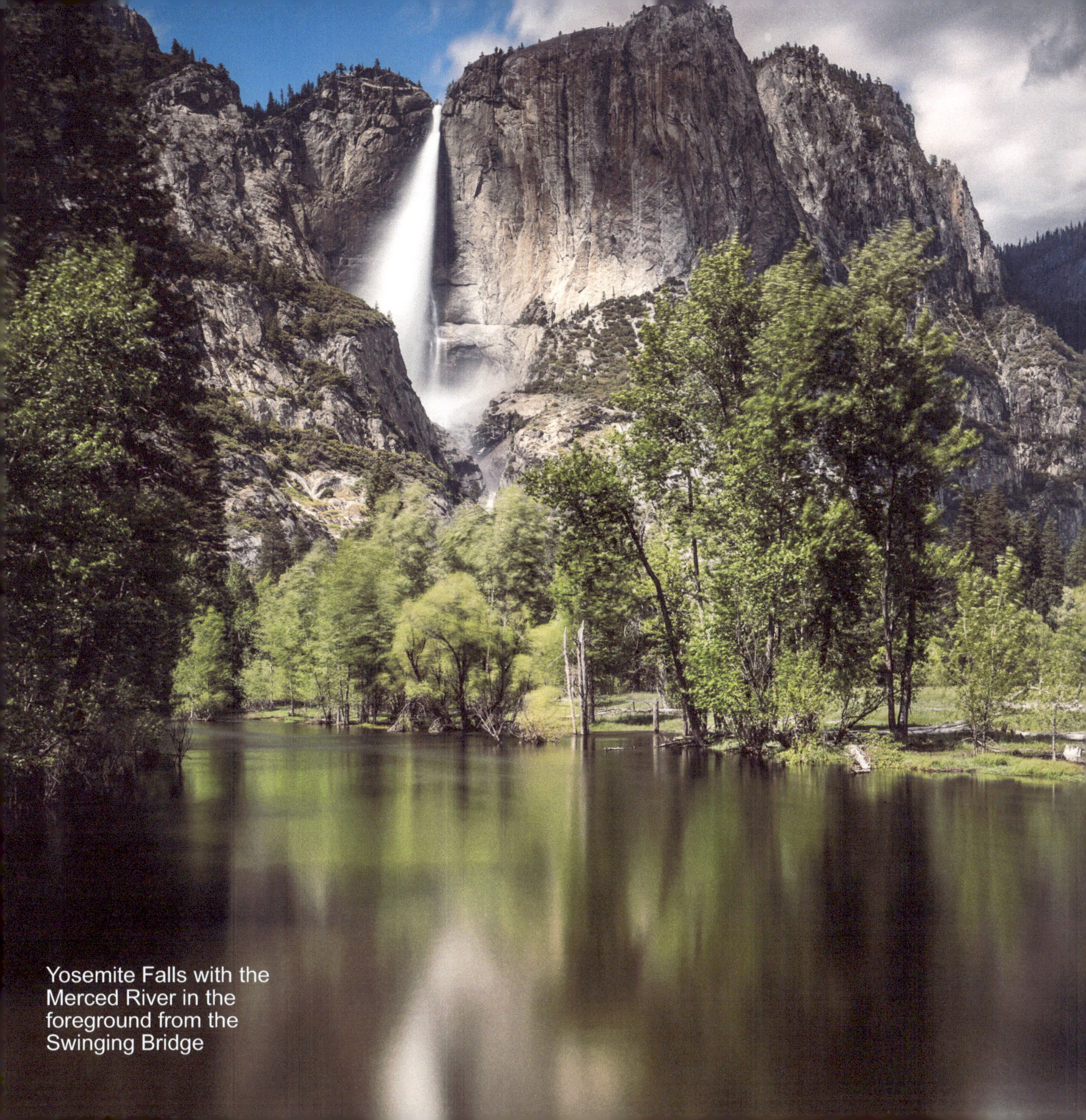

Yosemite Falls with the
Merced River in the
foreground from the
Swinging Bridge

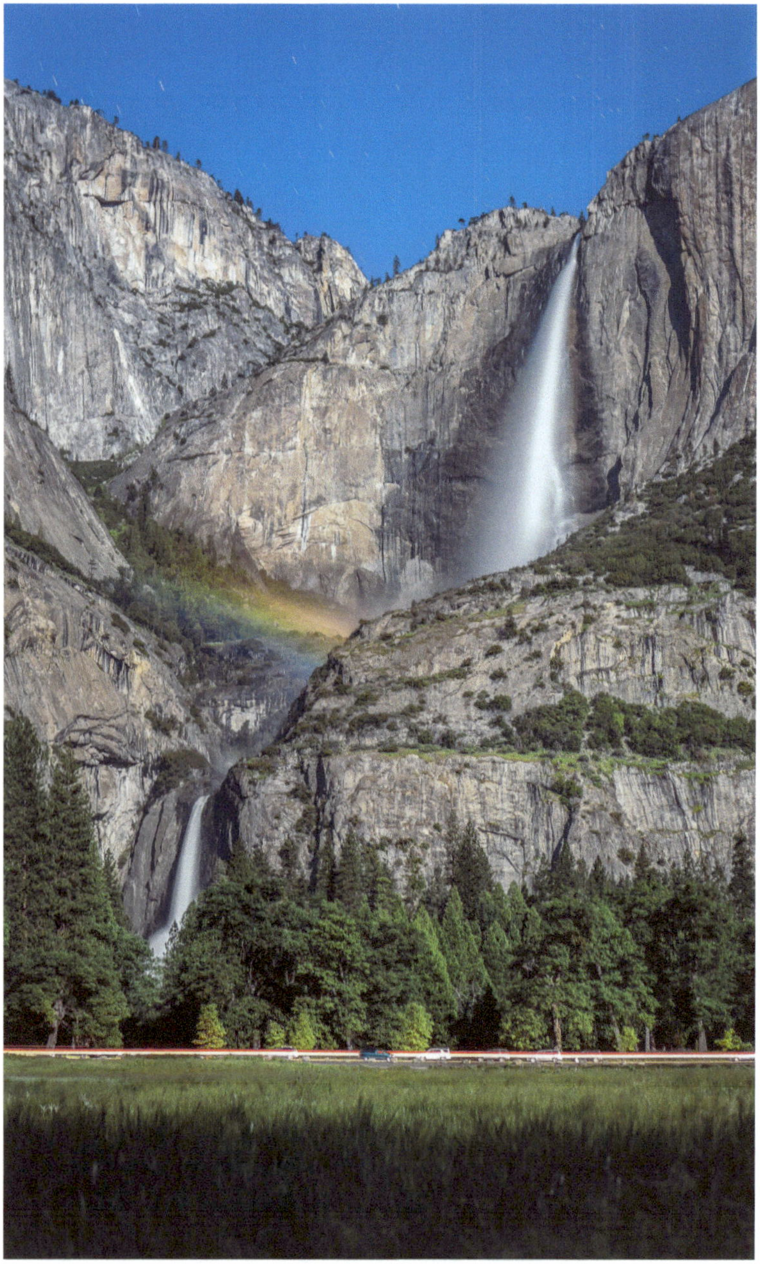

Yosemite Falls moon bow
under a full moon

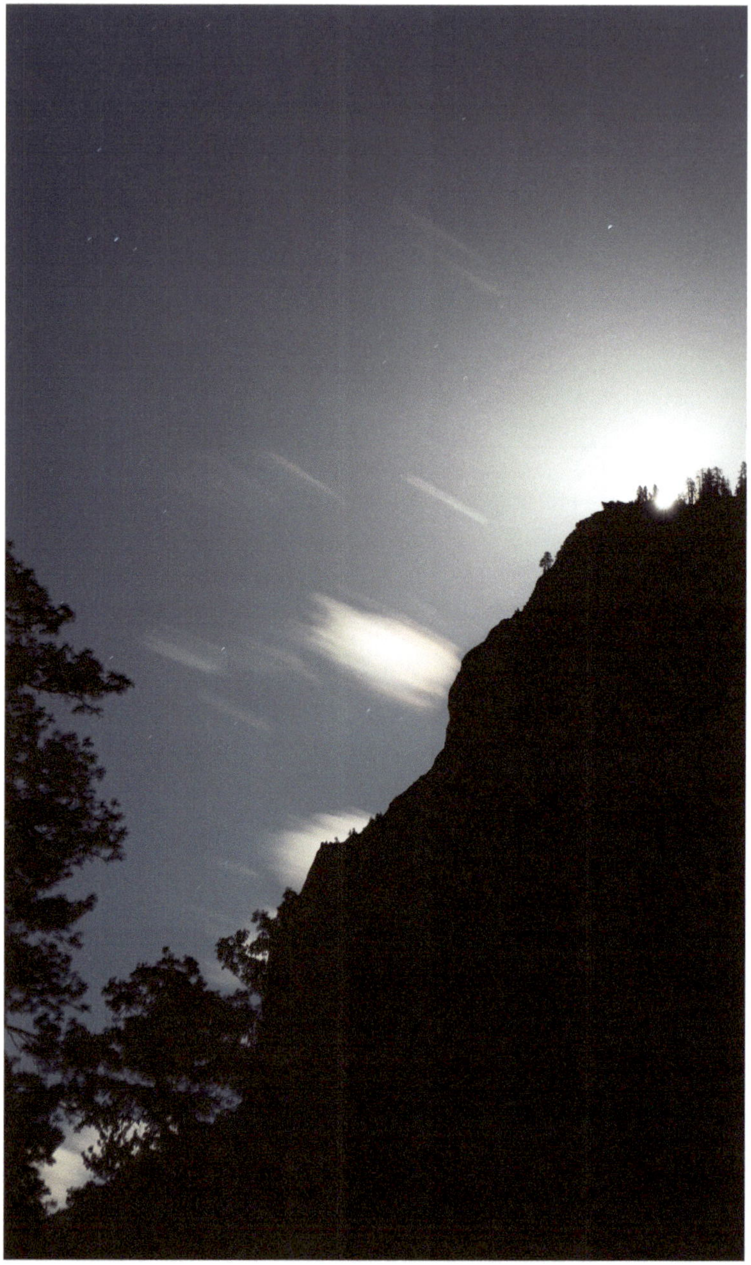

A full moon rises from behind Glacier Point

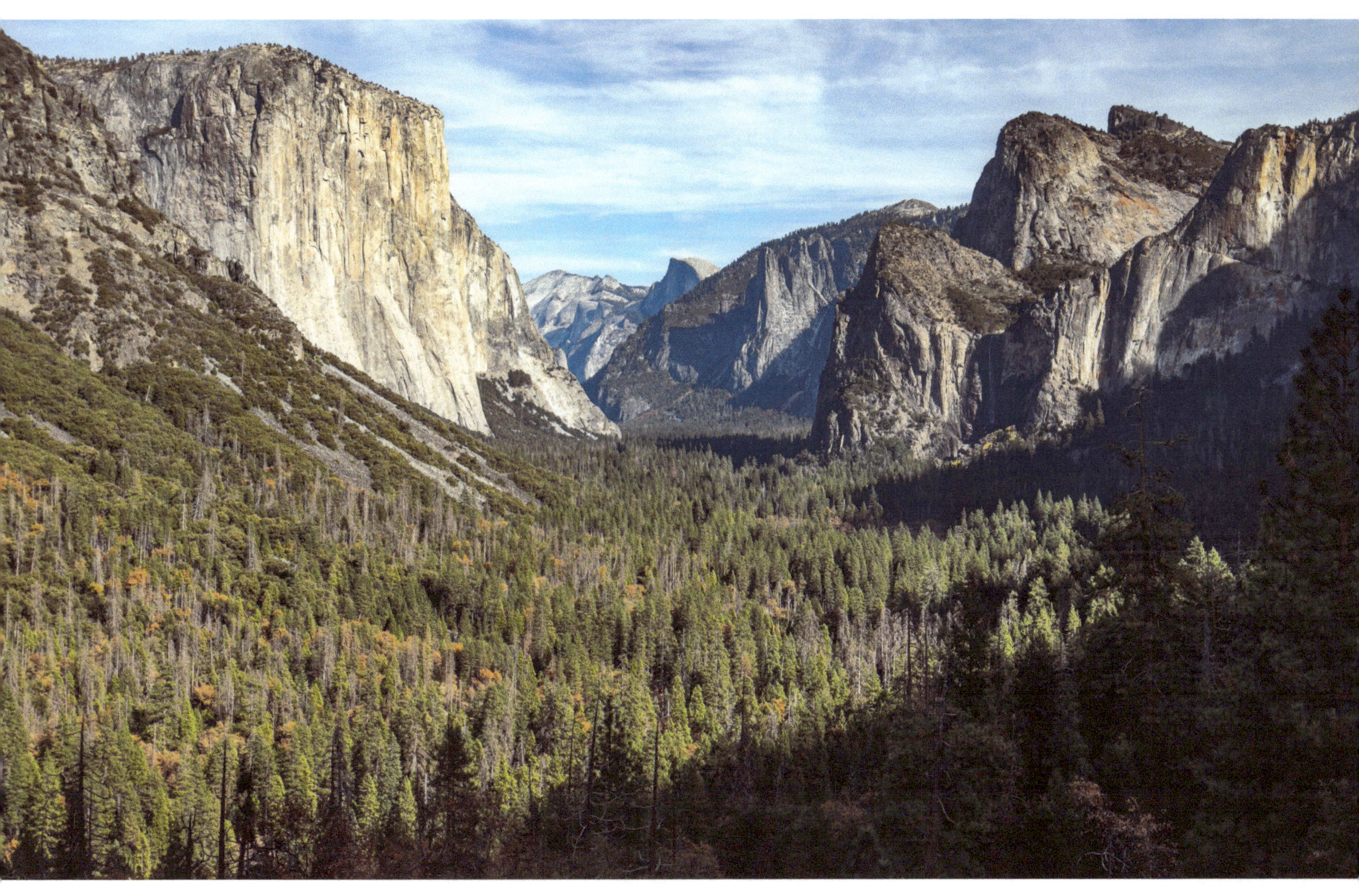

Tunnel View in the late fall

Fall brings cold, short days, fewer visitors and lots
of color to Yosemite Valley

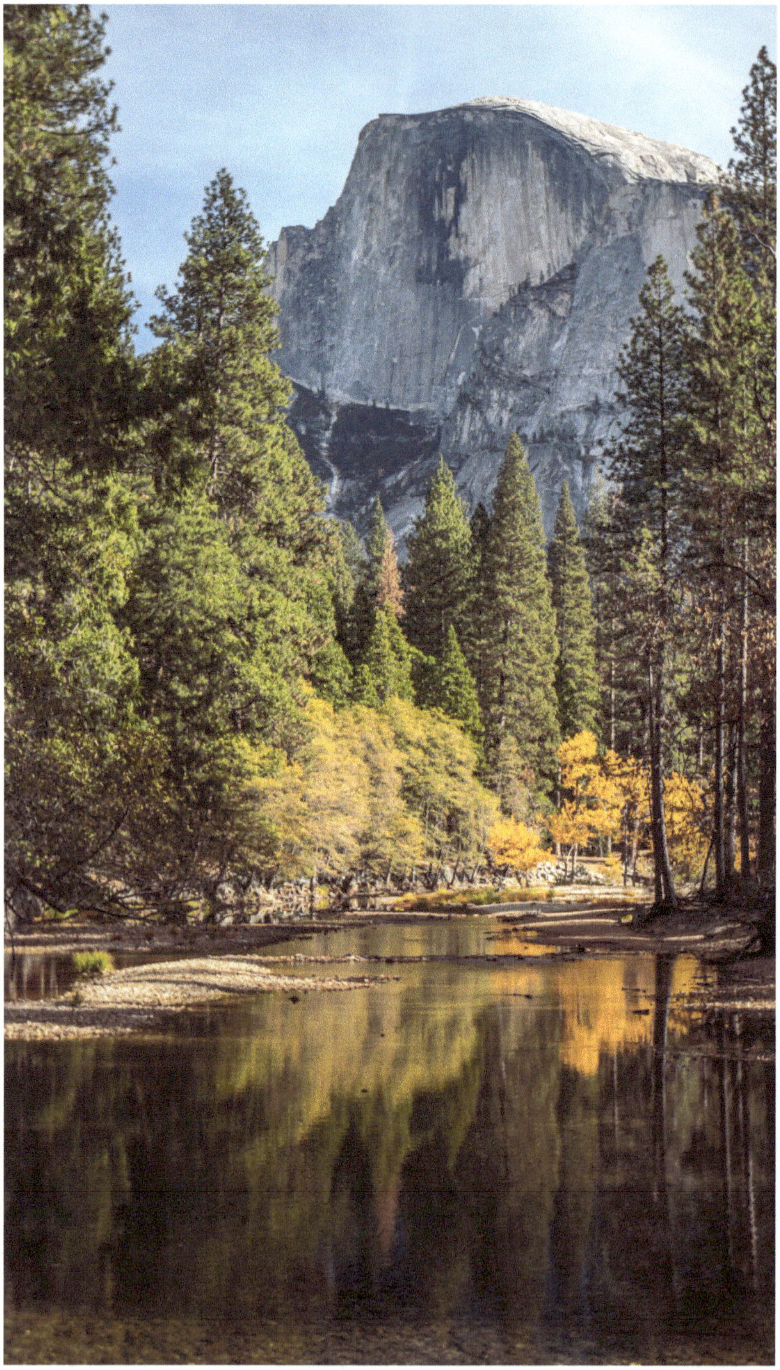

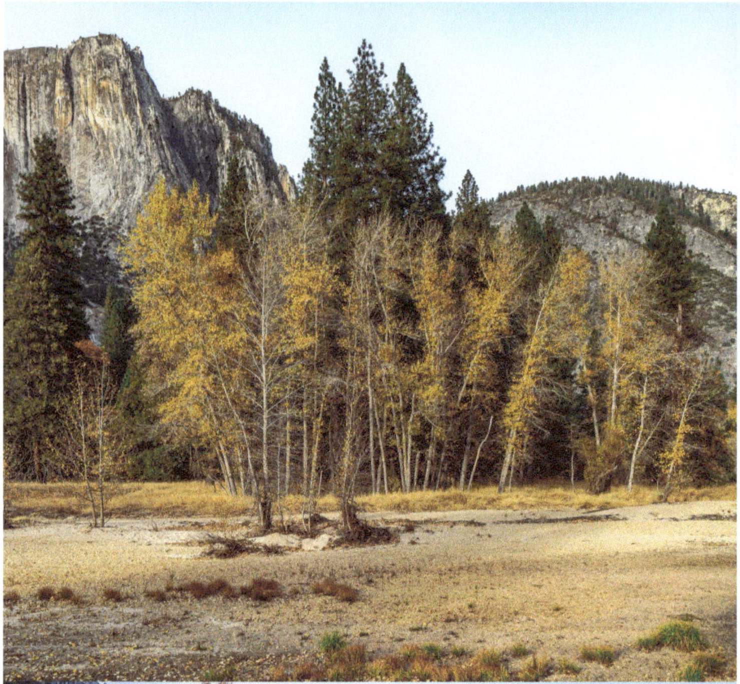

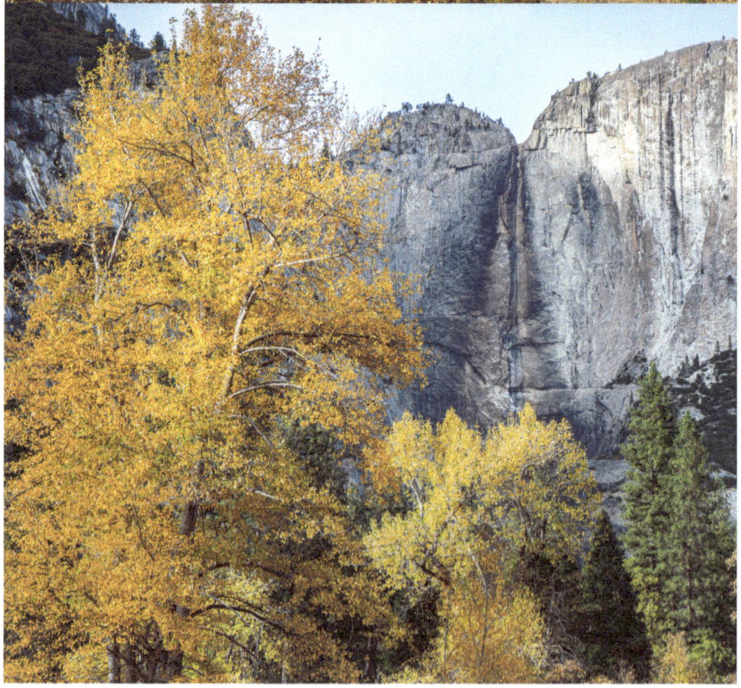

The cold brings colorful changes to the Valley

Waterfalls are drying up as the remaining snow pack is ready for a recharge
from the coming winter season

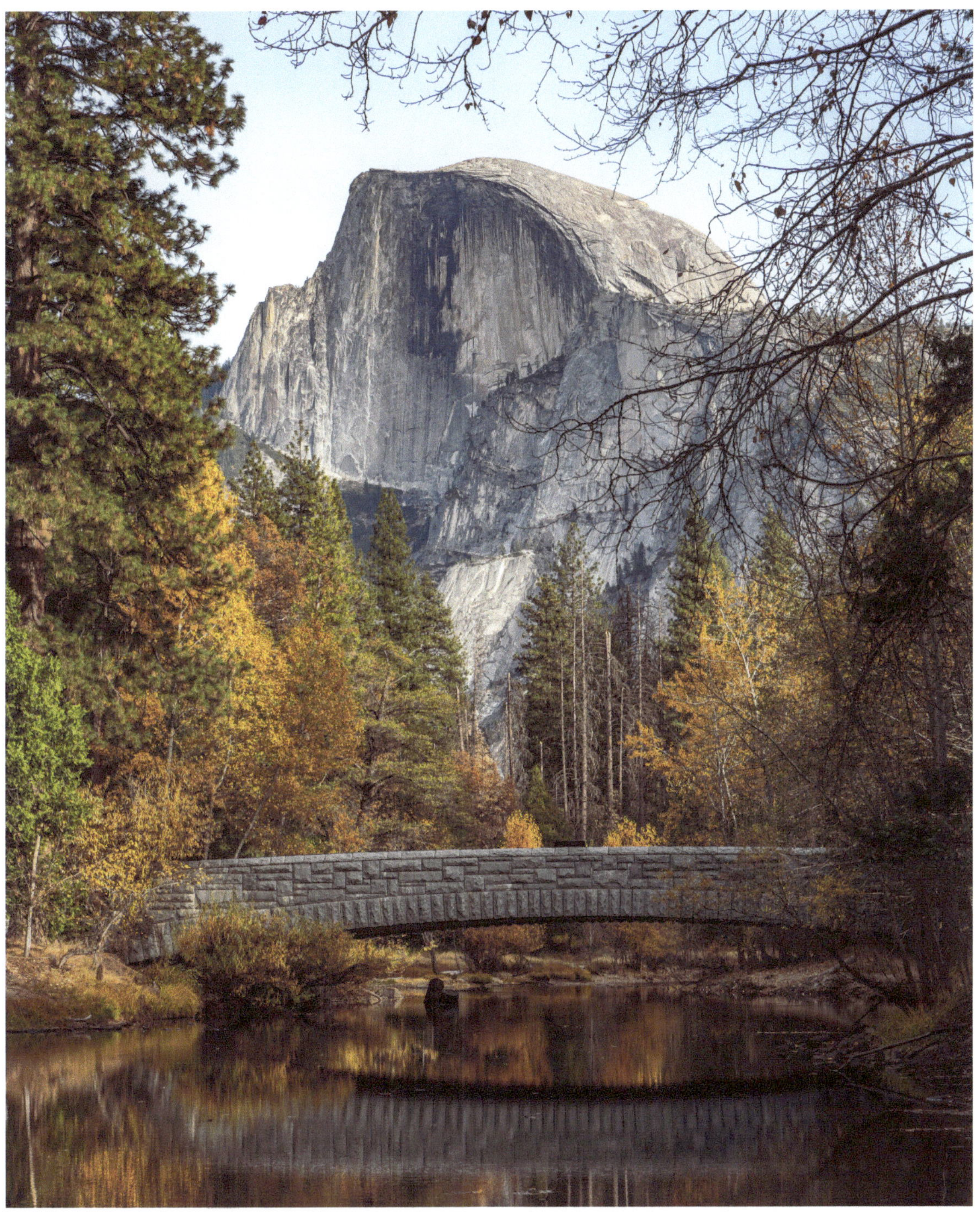

Half Dome and Sentinel Bridge

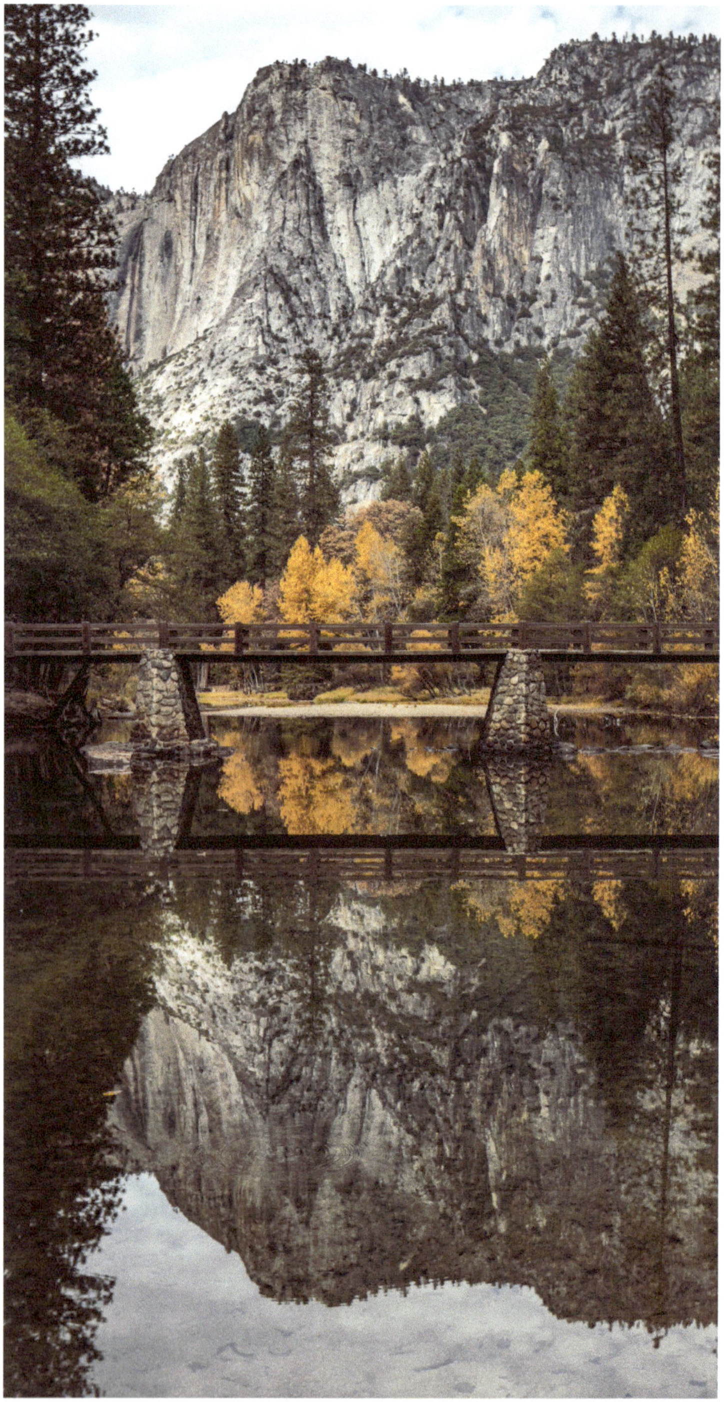

The bridge at Housekeeping Camp

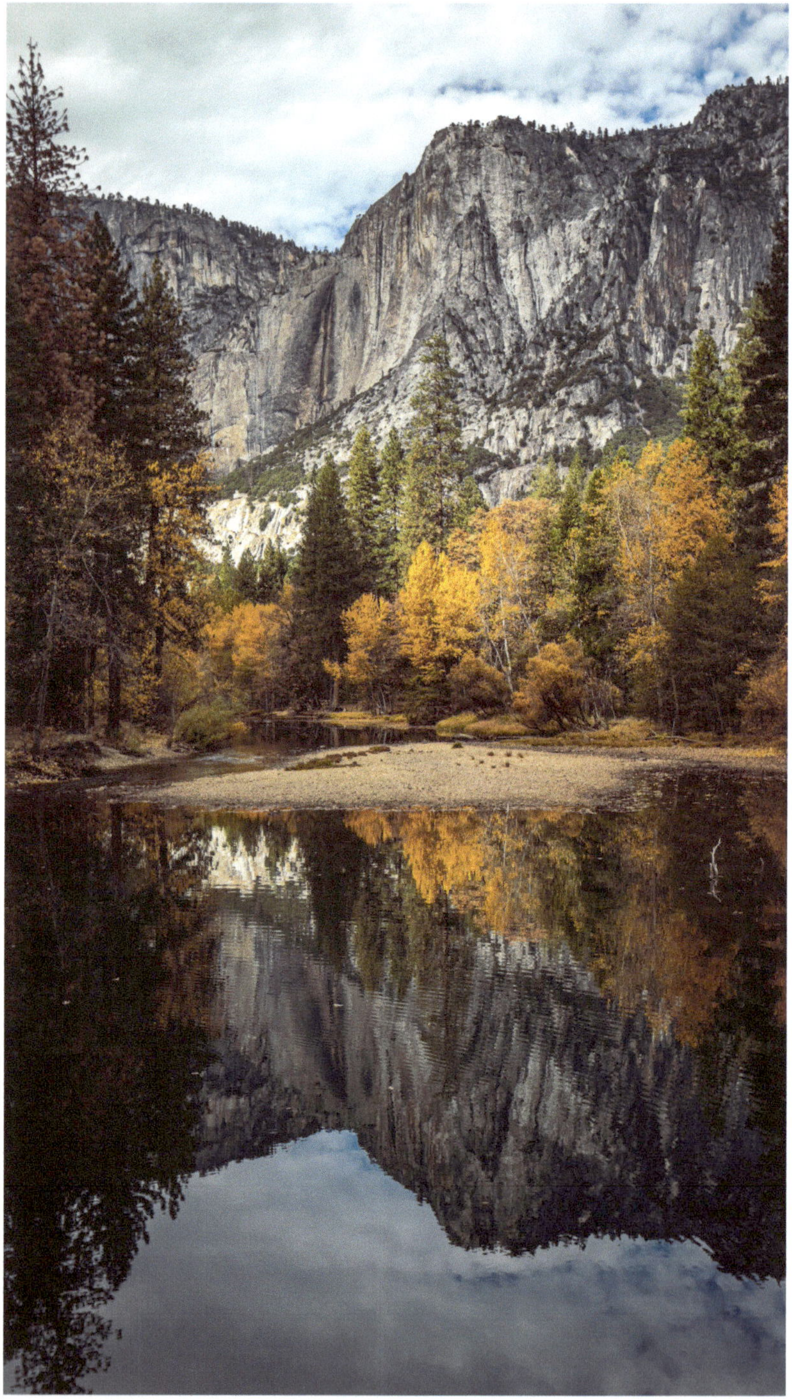

The Merced River gets calm and quiet near the end of fall and creates mirror-like reflections

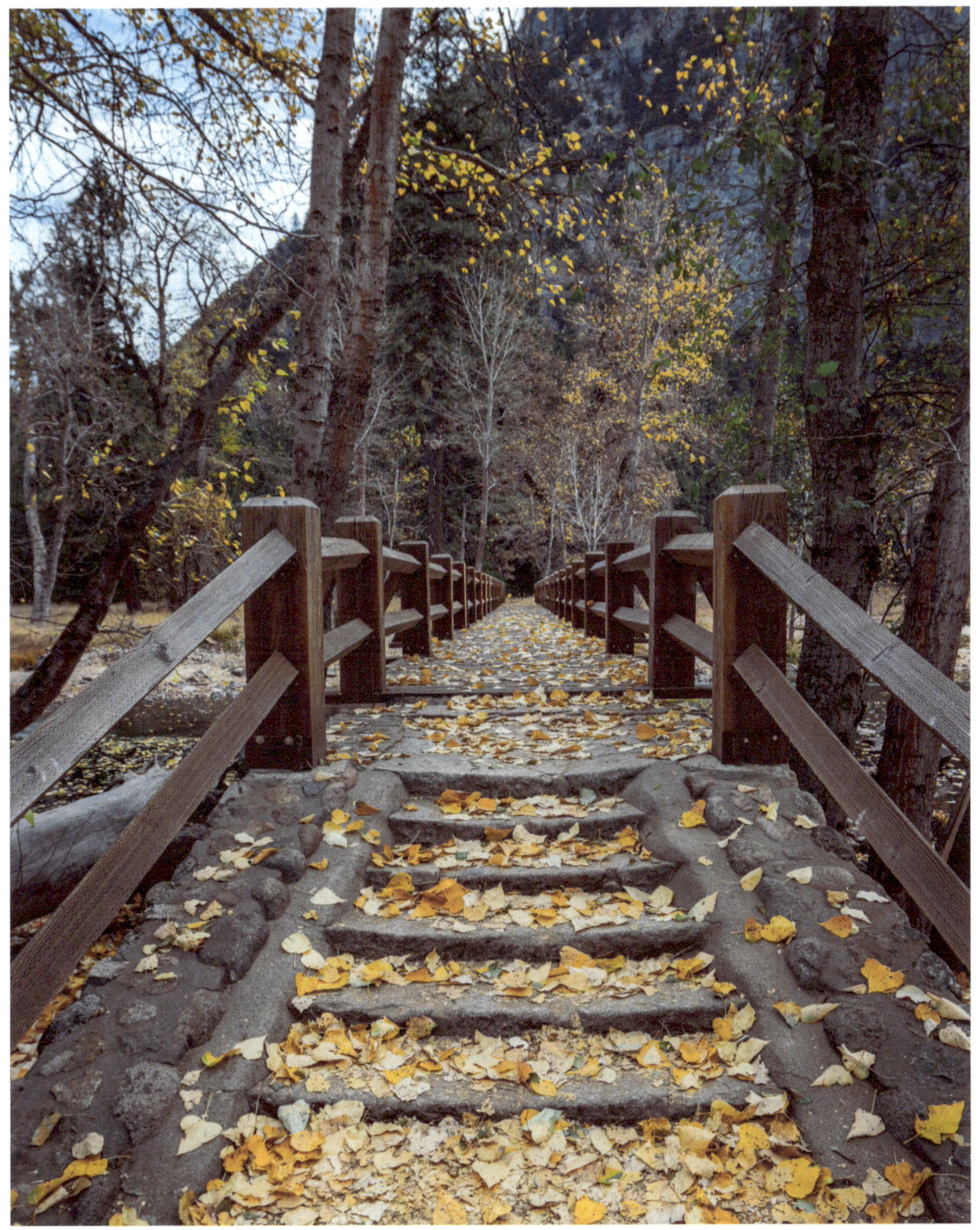

Superintendent's Bridge as the last of the fall colors come off the trees

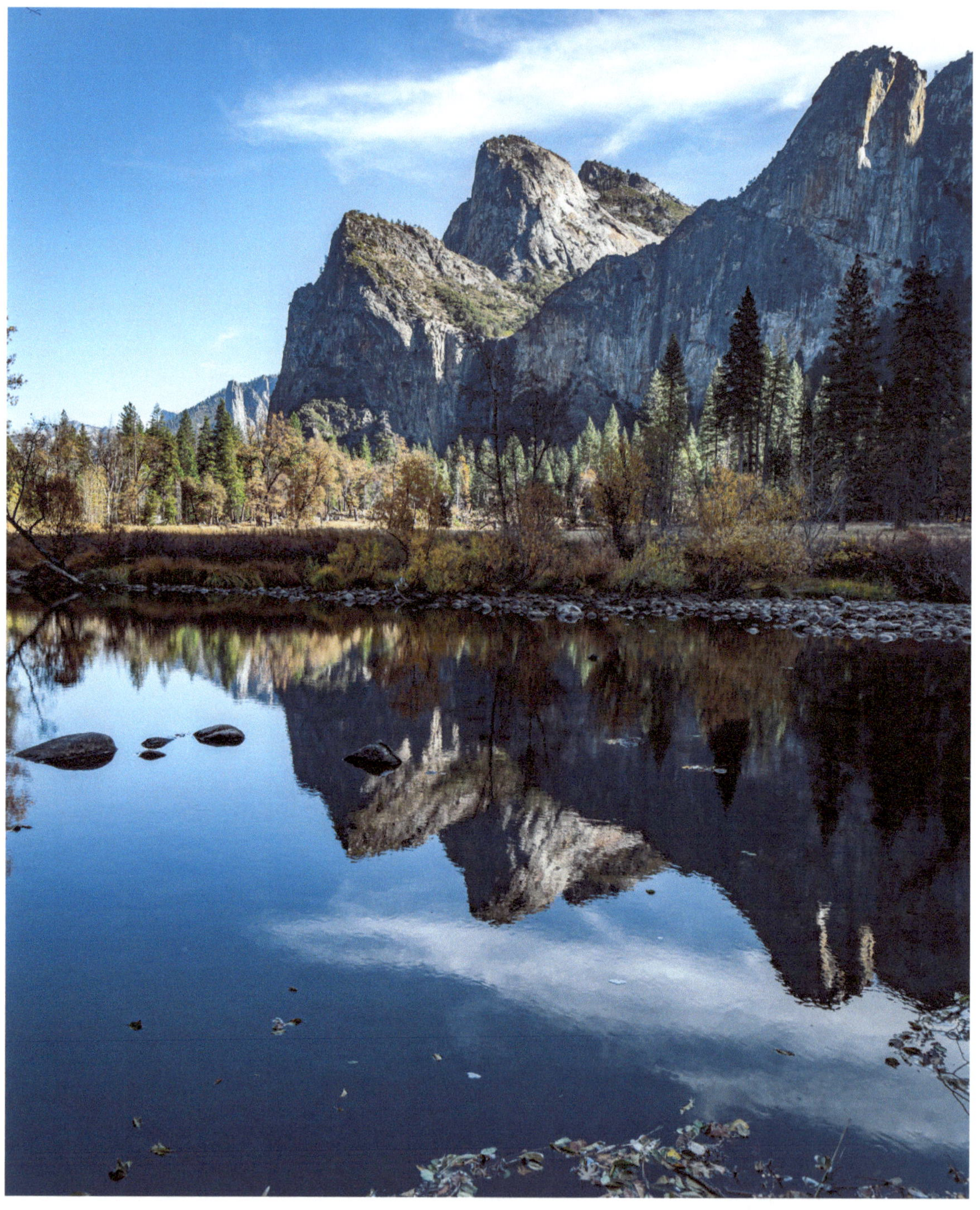

The Three Brothers standing over the calm Merced River
as seen from Valley View

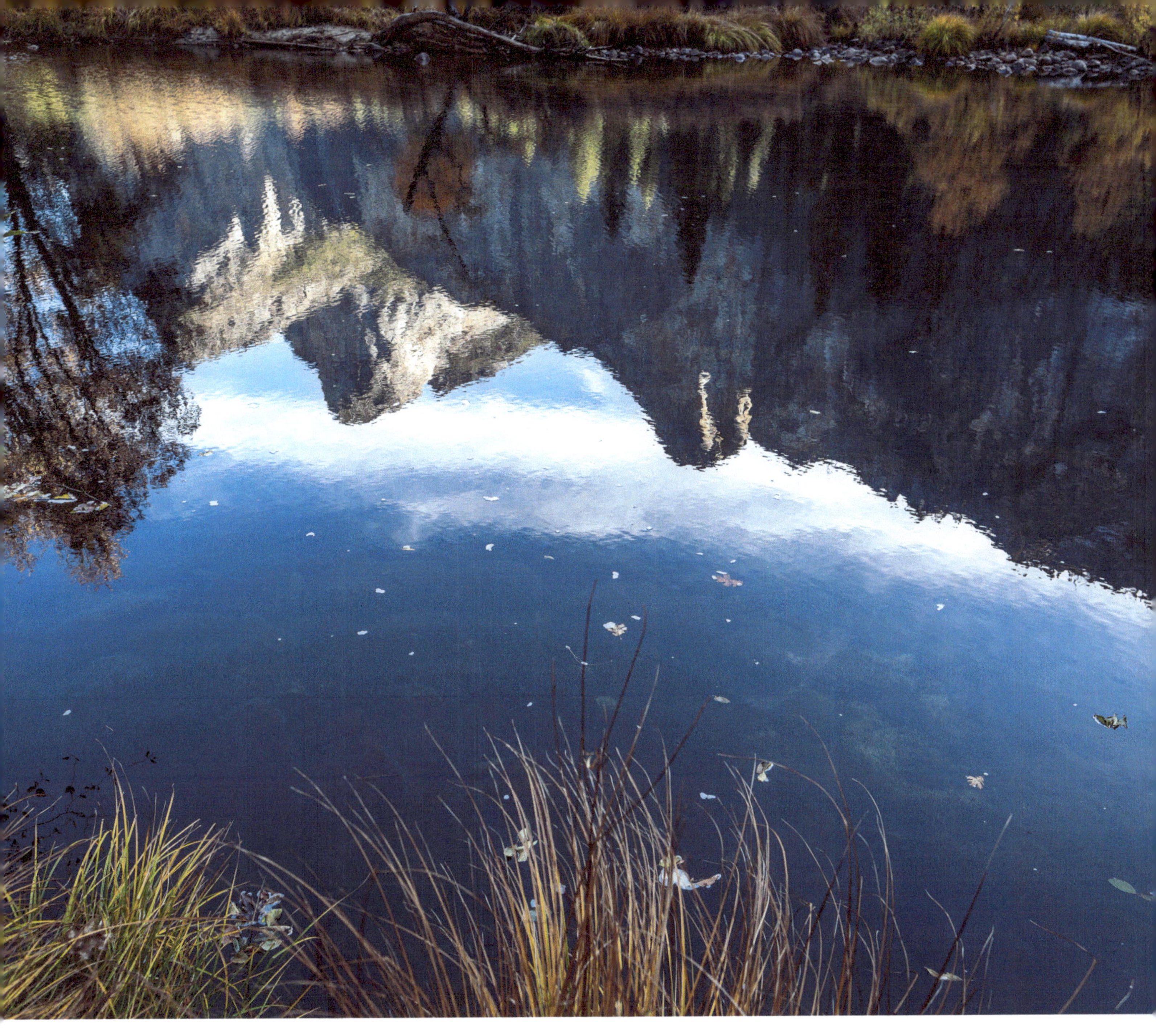

The Last of the fall colors float down the Merced River as the valley
prepares for the first snow of the season

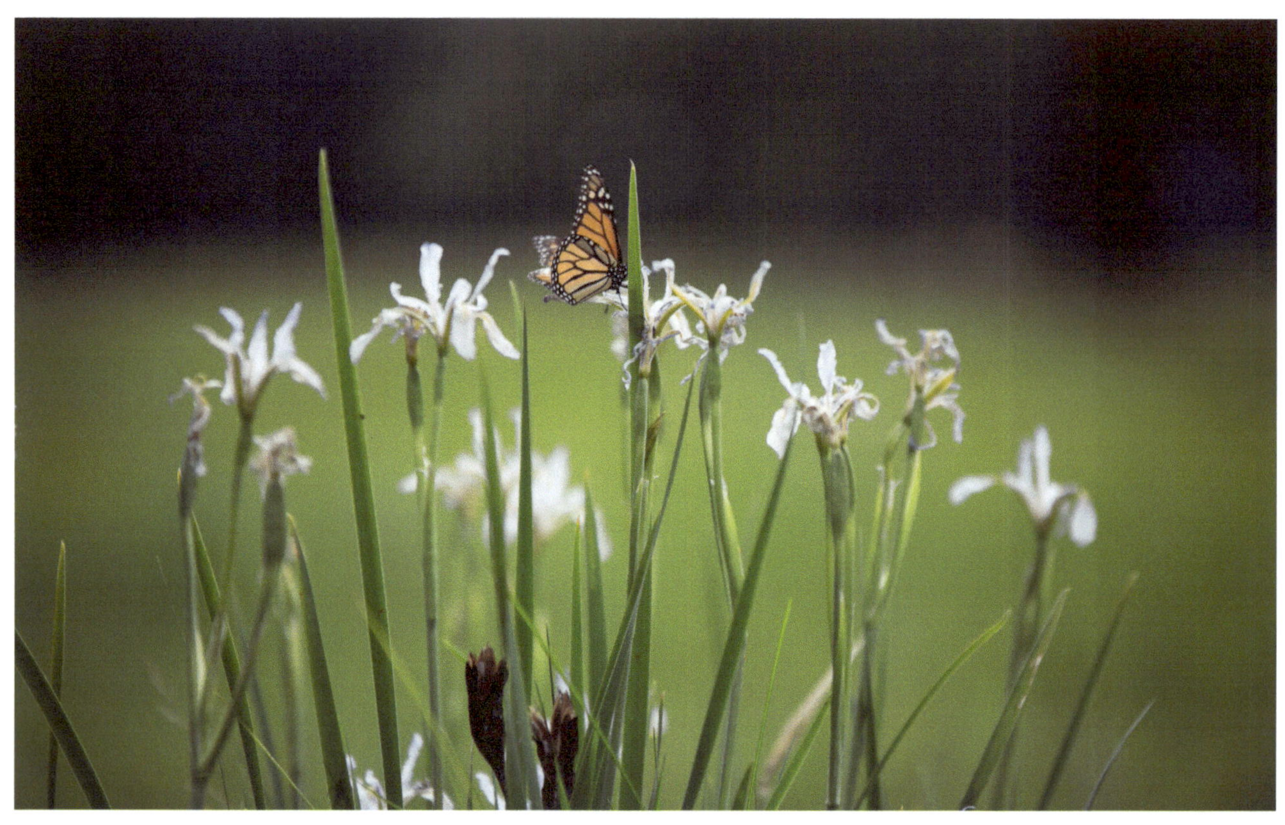

Yosemite: Capturing Nature's Grandeur